The Salon Punk

The Salon Punk
Alan Forrest Smith
Published By Master And Man Books

ISBN: 978-5136-2861-5

The author of this book does not offer any kind of life advice, action
advice or directional advice. The intent of this publication is to simply
share observations of life, stories of a life and the result of actions
taken by an individual. The author assumes no responsibility for any
action taken by the reader.

The SALON PUNK

●

Alan Forrest Smith

Published By Master And Man Books

ISBN: 978-5136-2861-5

Table of Contents

An Introduction

I'm not sure why you'd want to read this book.

I can't make any great claims of taking over the hair-dressing world or winning endless hairdressing awards. I never had fifty stylists breaking endless records and I never had a salon that turned over millions in pounds in haircuts or hairdressing services.

Yet looking back at my 17-years as a salon owner I feel did do something pretty amazing in my own little world of hairdressing that you as a salon owner can look at and feel inspired by.

Before I did that amazing little thing I had to accept this one thing about my life as a hairdresser and salon owner. It was this.

Being a great hairdresser was and will never enough to create a successful hairdressing business. It just isn't. Your great and successful salon business only arrives when you begin letting the public know you are a great hairdresser with a great salon.

It's about knowing; managing, aiming, pushing, directing and marketing your salon in ways that could cost you nothing and give you everything. It's also about finding and using systems that are actually proven to work and work fast in a salon like yours.

And I know that because I've done that for many salons as a mentor and also done that for my own salons between 1989 and 2003.

I know for an absolute certainty that there are powerful things that must be done daily to make sure you have a hair salon business that is a success and that in turn gives you a much happier life. Happiness comes from doing the things in life you really feel the need to do. Your salon business either supports that or might actually be preventing that because of the lack of results.

If you are not making enough money or unable to cover your bills or pay your stylists or even unable to pay yourself – you'll have a huge problem and that huge problem will make you unhappy with your life. A lack of money when you're working hard can be a real killer. Yet it is fixable and can be fixed fast.

I had to slowly and sometimes painfully learn the art of turning my salon into a real business. A business that could give me the kind of life I wanted. The life I wanted then was really a life built around a young family that needed to be fed, looked after and nourished. I had to create a business that would do just that. That's exactly what I eventually did. I could not afford for it to fail. Failure for me really meant no food on the table that really was my personal bottom line.

Eventual success in my salons gave me the ability to build my own stunning five-bedroomed converted barn on a farm, have around a one acre plot of garden with it's own orchard and space for my kids to play around and have the time and money to be able to live a more enhanced life as a hairdresser.

So when I say I am not sure why you want to read this book I am saying that because although it seems obvious to me now what to do with a salon to get it packed, to get busy and to be number one I suppose the truth is it was far from obvious in the early days for me (1985 - 2003). I made mistakes, plenty of them. Some mistakes were huge and almost cost me my salon and salons on more than one occasion. I will share those stories with you as you read along.

Yet, after 17-years with my salons and the hairdressing business I discovered, learned, uncovered and found some of the most incredible ways to make sure not only did we all stay busy but the phone rang constantly, the appointment book was packed and we even had a long list of clients waiting for a last minute appointment. This was an incredible achievement for a school drop-out, ex-landscape gardener and punk rocker to hit the top slot in a town of 35 very established salons.

Anyway, be sure of this. Whatever you are going through in your salon right now is pretty normal. Even the salon stars of this world have troubles and issues that would leave you jaw-dropped in total disbelief if you knew them. I know, I've worked with some of these guys and seen it first hand in the biggest to the smallest of salons. It is normal. It is fixable and can be fixed faster than you will know right now.

So this book is about my own experiences, my stories, my moments and also it is about real salon issues, it's about turning your hair salon into a real business that will give you the happier life I know you deserve for yourself, your family and your future.

Are you ready for that?

Ready?

Who Is Alan Forrest Smith

I am Alan Forrest Smith.

I did my first haircut when I was around 14 years of age although my own love of hair began with David Bowie and Ziggy Stardust. I was just 10-years old. I insisted my mother cut my hair like David Bowie. Mum wasn't a hairdresser but did cut peoples hair. She didn't want to cut off my feather cut but eventually with a huge poster of David Bowie sellotaped to the back of the kitchen door she did it. I went to school the next day and in a sea of 70s feather cuts I stood out like a sore thumb. The walk around A-block that day felt like a walk to my own death. It almost was and got beat up at least 5-times that first day as David Bowie.

Next it was 1977. Punk rock had arrived. I loved The Clash, The Damned and The Sex Pistols and the entire rule breaking of my new label - punk.

During my punk phase I have no idea how but I became the allocated hair cutter amongst my pals it just happened. I think I saw mum doing this all the time at homes so just assumed I could do it. Old carpet scissors in hand and away we go.

One day I cut my pal Georges hair into a Mohawk. I then bleached then coloured his hair purple with crazy colours. Not long after this his dad walked into the bedroom and saw what I had done. He went nuts and after trying to catch me to hit me for defacing his son I had to jump out of an upstairs window to escape a hiding from a man forty plus years older than me. I loved George's new purple hair and spikes! Thank god I also survived the jump of 14 f.t. from his bedroom window to cut away another day.

At 15-years of age I was ill and spent 3 months in bed with Hepatitis. I never went back to school I was just too sick. I hated school anyway. Finally I got a job as a gardener at the local council. After three-years as a landscape gardener digging holes and being freezing cold in winters I decided to drop out from that and study hairdressing.

By 1982 I had completed my college hair training with flying colours. I left early because I thought I was amazing. I wasn't, I was terrible. I actually had the best distinction results that the college had ever had at that time. I've no idea how as I had never passed an exam in my life and left school early. The only subject I surpassed in was Drama lessons!

After endless salon jobs, endless hair disasters on clients and endless firings the only option for me was to maybe open my own salon as I was totally unemployable and still am. I really hadn't given a lot of thought about owing my own salon, it really happened accidently.

During a haircut in a tiny kitchen in Cheshire where a dog kept trying to bite my ankle the client asked me if I would like to rent one of his small new shops he was about to build? I thought it was an OK idea and before I knew it I was signing a piece of paper I hadn't properly read committing myself to seven-year shop lease.

Finally, I opened my first salon in 1989 and charged the princely sum of £6.95 for a cut and blow because that is what everyone else was charging. That single decision almost destroyed my business, as I will explain later.

I've also employed hundreds of hairdressers, hundreds of juniors and god only knows how many others. Some I couldn't get rid of and others I loved having them with me. Others I would have paid happily anyone to take them off my hands. And others I fired only to face the wrath of father's, boyfriends and even a mother trying to kick down the front door of my home whilst I terrifyingly hid behind the sofa inside the safety of my little house.

I've written many books and words on business. My best-selling salon business manual is called Salon Extreme 21©. I wrote my first book for salons as an eBook in 1999 called Salon Column Builder. I'm flattered that is has been literally copy and pasted and stolen so many times by so many of the new 'experts' online as their own. Incredible people think it is OK to remove your name and add theirs as the author.

Anyway it is what it is.

I've also written many self-styled philosophy books. Escape from Zoomanity was my first book published in New York in 2012. I am Bastard I Am War, is another book. Deliberate Recreation, is yet another. There's over ten more available on Amazon. My publishers are both Morgan James Books and Master and Man Books as of writing.

And ... I was even a fundamentalist Christian ordained minister for over 20-years from 1985 – 2006.

I've written thousands of pages of blog posts since 1999 on subjects such as hairdressing, business and anti-political and more controversial topics covering, life, sex, religion and more.

I've traveled around the globe on client invites to share the keys to success that I've collected over three decades plus years in business. I once flew to New Zealand and flew back home like a madman right after the talk. The trip took 36-hours but felt like a month on that plane.

I've also lectured in Australia, Asia, USA, and Europe and of course even in my beloved Scotland. Once a well-known jewelry company in Melbourne flew me all the way to their shop to give them advice and help them solve a specific problem in their business. I solved it and gave them a small £30,000 and instant windfall from uncovered sales in the process.

I also spent two-weeks in the middle of the Amazonian jungle in Ecuador on an invite after I consulted and contributed to a forest saving charity. I swam in the Amazon River surrounded by huge Alligators and massive snakes. Clearly I was off my mind yet being told that the blind pink dolphins that were swimming around would protect me. It seemed to work. I was still scared witless if I'm honest; I doubt I would do that again!

I worked outside the hair industry and advised and consulted in maybe over 400 industries but I have been responsible for sales going well into the hundreds of millions of pounds from my strategic work in businesses inside and outside the salon business.

Big multi-million pound businesses like the 2nd biggest security firm in the UK, small start-up or struggling businesses like small local salons, post offices, florists, car showrooms, cosmetic companies, landscaping and even cafes and even those in the middle that just want more results from their business.

I suppose you could say I know what I'm doing when it comes to business and building salon businesses fast.

Yet, time and time again I am always drawn back to my roots that lie deep in hairdressing. And, why shouldn't I? For me it's where everything really began in business. I did some cool stuff with my own three salons. I was never the mighty Sassoon or Toni and Guy but in the town we felt bigger and better than even the biggest of them.

I've done a ton of very cool things with other salons probably just like yours like giving one salon owner 404 new clients from a single campaign or another salon owner that generated over £1,400 after doing a simple tweak in his salon marketing.

Another I saved from certain closure with an increase they called "INSANE" in just 23-days and another where I increased their new clients by over 586.3% and helped one salon owner to give his graduate an opportunity to get them on the shop floor. The graduate went from just £250 per week to £1,700 per week over just 10-weeks!

I am considered a results driven and absolutely without a doubt – proven - expert with strategic business building within and outside our industry, as you'll see as you read through.

Just to stress, I'm not showing off but as a simple truth is I know a lot about a lot but I know almost everything there is to know about running a hairdressing business or turning a hair salon into a real business. That is just a simple fact supported by results.

Saying that all of this always leads me to ask one question regardless of the business I am working with.

Your business, your hairdressing salon, it either works or it doesn't. There is no middle ground. And who wants middle ground when you can take the high ground? And what does it mean to say 'it works?' Does it give you what you want from life and it is making you the money you deserve for such a huge commitment?

If it isn't well it isn't working is it?

And as hairdressers we are not really designed or trained to run a real business in a really strategic or higher demand way. We are creative, most of us are crazy and most of us want everything from what we are creating. It's the buzz, it's the fix, and it's the addiction to our industry that makes our skills and results so interesting. But as far as being a 'businessperson' most of us just don't have that training.

The only real problem with that is when we are salon owners it can be so easy for us to do what we think or are told is right yet the actual reality of having a truly profitable hair salon business can be very different. That difference can soon manifest itself in huge outstanding invoices, growing debts and staff that is just out of control (I've lost count of the amount of stylists I've seen almost destroying salons).

Yet here's the good news. It doesn't have to be like that at all. It doesn't have to be high pressure. It doesn't have to be you standing at the edge of the cliff waiting to jump or be pushed off.

Recently, I worked with a salon that has only been open 9-months as I write this. When they came to me you certainly got the impression that everything was lost. Spiraling debts, staff out-of-control and more. After doing what you will read about in the book not only did I turn every aspect of their salon around with them they saw crazy extreme increases like new clients up by 2033.3%, average bills up from £16 to well over £72, sales of Olaplex up by 2,200%, client visits up by 85.2% and their actual salon income up by a massive 233.7%. This was after WEEKS not years of working with me.

In money terms that meant over a 28-day period I gave the salon owners their best week ever in January and increased their turnover from around £1,700 to just under £6,000 per week.

Like I said, not only do I know what I am doing but also you are about to read how I did and do those things in this book.

Finally ...

I am sharing a lot of my own hairdressing back-story and experiences. This will help you to truly understand where it all comes from. I think you'll relate to a lot of what I am putting down here from your own salon perspective and daily business.

For me as I write this book is about possibility because I've come to learn that more than what you might be thinking is possible. Even the most outrageous of thoughts are possible. I've seen it. I've done it. I helped others do it.

A successful salon is possible for you.

And it's true, I'm a PUNK that grew up on rebellion and fighting the systems, I don't know why I just can't help it.

So it arrived ... The Book ... THE SALON PUNK

I hope you enjoy reading this book as much as I enjoyed pulling back the memories and writing it down for you.

1963: A Hairdresser Is Born

Here's how I got here.

I was born in 1963 in Scotland in a place named Leith. Leith is in Edinburgh. This is the most important place in Scotland. Apparently!

By the time 1977 had arrived so had The Sex Pistols, The Clash, The Damned and a new teenage rage called Punk Rock. I remember seeing the Sex Pistols on a TV show named 'So It Goes'. It was the 28th August 1976. This TV moment blew me away. I was changed forever. An old TV hippy named Tony Wilson and the anti-hippies also known as the Sex Pistols together. They delivered a song that was to outrage the nation. The song was Anarchy In The UK. I loved it. Dad hated it and wanted to smash the TV.

Punk rock still leaves its residue in most that were part of the punk movement. This includes me. It really was to define an early version of who I was and how I thought about my world. I didn't realise but realise now how much lyrics can affect a young mind. My mind was slowly being indoctrinated with an attitude and self-belief that most rules were there to be broken and the possibility that everything was now possible. In justice and dishonesty was also part of the mantra. The truth is nothing ever changes.

Punk rock affected my whole life and my whole ethic towards life and business especially the hairdressing business. It was always asking me to question everything.

The attitude, the possibilities, the rule breaking, the no bullshit approach so when most say it can't be done I would simply ignore, break every rule and make it happen.

Which of course takes me onto my first real business, which was hairdressing. For me hairdressing and punk rock were brothers in arms, so intertwined and complete in every form of expression. In my gang of pals I had become the one who had enough confidence to attempt cut and colour everyone's hair like Sid Vicious and dye it like Jonny Rotten despite the fact I had no idea what I was doing. This was my own introduction into 'hands-on' or 'learn as you go' hairdressing, touching hair, doing things with hair and using hair to make a statement and even create a new attention grabbing lifestyle.

No rules were needed. All I knew and my pals knew was to be a punk rocker we had to smash the rules and constrictions and demands of society or formality.

For me my own personal rules in business were built around this very idea of no-rules yet it was an idea without too much thought, more intuitive or reactionary.

This idea for business was so deeply engrained that most problems faced by others in their salon businesses never felt like real unsolvable problems for me. Being a punk was being anti-establishment and anti most things. In business I feel the same.

I'll explain more as I go through my story. I also wanted to share how my own 70s hippy and kaftan wearing mother shaped the way I do my salon business. Her influence and her attitude to make things happen are undeniably unshakeable. She's probably more punk rock than she'll ever know she just doesn't know it.

1973: My First 'First' Business

It's back to 1973 and I am just 10-years old. I am a Scottish immigrant that has moved to England for a better life with my family. I am of course cute (nothing changed) but my accent is strong and I stand out as do my family. We live on a council estate that is run by the home office for prison warders. My father is a prison warder. He actually spent more years in a prison than most of the worst offenders.

The electric goes off and on all the time because of strikes as the socialists are in power. All the kid's parents are all at work whilst we spend day after day just playing and looking after ourselves. We ride our Raleigh chopper bikes around the estate pretending to be Hells Angels or even better Evil Knevil.

The music of the Bay City Rollers, David Bowie, Marc Bolan and Rod Stewart can be heard blaring from house windows as we ride up and down the streets only to park up and then to steal apples from Mr. Clare's garden on the corner.

The more we ride the more we damage our bikes. It wasn't uncommon for a bike to look like a real wreck just month after Christmas after all not only were we hells Angels in training we are also spotty 10-year old Evil Kevil's and could pull any stunt from a wheelie to flying over 4-6-foot gaps and landing on a ramp at the other side.

My purple chopper got so scratched I decided that it would be a cool idea to get some paint in a spray can and repaint it. Behind our house were old car garages we would break into all the time by climbing through the broken but very dangerous asbestos roofs. We were never stealing we were simply being commandos avoiding being seen by imaginary spotlights.

I found some orange spray paint and put it in my also army kit bag that I had also requisitioned (stolen) from the old army base at Taylors industrial estate where we would visit on a regular basis. On a side note we all wore bullet belts, grenade pouches, gun holsters and even jungle machetes we also took from the old army base. Only those that got the gas mask were seen as commanding officers and that was always the very ugly boy named 'Gaz'! The soldiers had gone long before we arrived so it really felt it was fine.

Anyway, after stealing the paint we sneaked out of the old garage then we all went home where I decided to strip down my battered bike and paint it in our kitchen. When my parents got home Mum almost killed me for half painting the cooker orange.

Once my bike was re-painted in orange and rebuilt I was to go on a new mission the following day where we had all decided to dig a tunnel under the old railway like on the Great Escape with Steve Mc Queen. Everyone would meet outside the housing estate pub and then ride out but this morning was to be different.

When I arrived all the boys stopped and asked about my now orange bike. They couldn't believe how cool it was. They wanted the same. One at a time I took their bikes back with me and painted the bikes with my random cans of paint I had 'also borrowed and got paid cash on delivery.

I charged fifty pence per bike. My stock cost nothing. Maybe I painted twenty bikes at that time. Mark stole his fifty pence from the Milk round he used to do. I've no idea where the rest of the boys got theirs. Suddenly I was the richest kid on the council estate so I went and bought myself an air rifle where I began to shoot my pals in the legs whilst lying under a car with my face covered in black oil from under the car. I really wanted to be a sniper not a commando.

At ten years of age I had learnt a critical lesson in business. I didn't know that at the time but it was a rule that stuck with me until this day and it is this.

People will buy what they WANT to buy, what they are ready to buy if you put it in front of them.

They wanted painted bikes.

I painted the bikes.

1974: The Sewing Machine and Ziggy Stardust

It can be a strange thing to see a kid that thinks he is a sniper dressed in flared jeans wearing a David Bowie t-shirt using a sewing machine but that's what happened. The sewing machine was there; I was bored and curious so I started using it.

I decided to sew together some bedding and make a parachute. I went into my room and removed my bed sheet. It was easy and my parachute worked. First, I jumped from the back wall, which was maybe six-foot high. Then tried trees that were just a little higher. Then finally my battalion decided it was time someone tried it by jumping off the roof and I mean the roof of the house.

Gaz – the crazy one - decided he would do it after all he was our leader. After climbing up the drainpipe at the side Gaz carefully got into position at the edge of the roof. The parachute was rolled up behind him and then he jumped. The parachute didn't open and Gaz broke his leg. We decided being grounds troops was the safer option so the parachute adventure ended. From there I made tents to go camping, sails for our battle ships on the local pond and flags for our rafts. I became a bit of an expert playing around on a sewing machine. Stick with these stories; they are all relevant to hairdressing.

The Bay City Rollers the Scottish pop band had become huge. They were from Edinburgh the same place I was from so I kind of wanted to be Les or Woody in my own way.

I had the jeans but no tartan on the jeans. The rollers and their fans always had tartan turn-ups or stripes down the side. I asked my mum to buy me a tartan scarf. I took the scarf, cut it up and sewed the tartan into my jeans.

The day I left my house to ride my chopper was the day I was inundated with orders for tartan turn-ups on jeans. I charged everyone a small amount – just £0.50p. Again I probably did around twenty pair of jeans and again I was a rich kid on a very poor council estate.

One day my father arrived home with his new prison officer uniform. The trousers always looked like they were two meters long so they needed to be adjusted. Dad asked me if I could do that for him. I told him yes and did the adjustment. He never paid me but suddenly he was bringing home trousers from all of his work pals to be adjusted. I did this off and on for years and once again was making money whilst all my pals were digging tunnels on the old railway hoping to reach re-enact the great escape.

I had what people wanted, I never had what I thought they might buy or I thought they might one day need. They were all happy to pay for what they wanted and I was the only person on the council estate giving them what they wanted.

1977: The Sex Pistols
And The Hairdresser

Punk rock reintroduced the skinny 'drainpipe' jean. The problem was you couldn't buy them then. I was fourteen-years old and I really wanted skinny's like Jonny Rotten or the Ramones. I had the skills with my sewing machine so I simple cut up my flares and stitched them back together into ultra-tight skinny's. Of course I also made skinny jeans for all of my pals ... supply and demand! Jeans for cash!

My hair was still longish again for a punk and this was a problem. I again asked mum for a new haircut. So I gave her a photo of Jonny Rotten the singer from the Sex Pistols and asked her to cut it like that. She did, it was a mess and I loved it.

Now I wanted it coloured. My best pal John and myself went to Clippers salon in our village. John went purple and I went red and yellow. Now I had to go home and see what the reaction would be. I rode home on my little motorbike (Yamaha FS1E), walked into the house but I didn't take off my helmet. After around twenty-minutes my dad asked why I hadn't taken it off and then demanded I remove it.

I was nervous; I knew dad would go nuts! I removed my helmet only to be faced by a large and heavy whack from my furious dad. I was banned from leaving the house until the colour grew out! The ban lasted a day or two.

All the boys were growing up now and all the boys also wanted to look cool, up to the minute and happening. When they saw my long hair cut short and spiked they wanted exactly the same. They asked if I could do it. I said sure. I had watched mum cutting hair so many times and it looked easy to me.

I started cutting all my pals hair. I even started coloring all their hair. I would charge a couple of pounds and it was still way cheaper than going to a hairdresser that hadn't caught up on trends. Once more I was the richest kid on the housing estate and my pals were still throwing their pocket money at me for haircuts.

I managed to buy a leather motorbike jacket like the ones wore by the Ramones from my new teenage wealth. It was cool and frankly I didn't really know what I was doing.

Nothing had really changed.

Everyone wanted skinny's and spiked hair. I gave them exactly what they wanted and they hand over their cash as a nice value exchange.

I didn't realise then but my lessons for business had been established very young and it was as simple as give people what they already want.

The punk rock adventure continued for sometime. I formed a punk band I named Clone Youth. We never got bigger than leaving Warrington in Cheshire but we did get a session on the very famous John Peel show on the BBC.

We wrote songs, recorded the songs on tapes, played gigs and guess what? People wanted Punk Bands in those days and punk songs. I gave them what they were already asking for but really I was chasing fame!

I was never truly a rich kid but I always had money in my pocket. I never asked for pocket money, never asked for clothing money, I never really asked for anything. I was making my own way by simply filling a demand or giving buyers what they wanted to buy.

And that's business right? Being in business for me is about getting paid. Not huge risks but simply finding what people are searching for, finding what people have already bought in their minds and supplying the demand for them. They get what they want and I get paid for giving it to them.

If there is no money in the drawer at the end of the week no one gets paid and no one gets fed. Yet for me it has always been just pure common sense that you give people what they want rather than trying force them to buy anything.

Looking back today the lessons in my young life were just absolutely huge. I had developed an ability to create my own income by sticking to a simple rule of demand. This would resurface once I opened my own hairdressing salon.

Today, so many hairdressing salons try far too hard to create new marketplaces. Chasing new clients with new services when the old clients are under serviced. Even Apple didn't create a new marketplace they tapped into emerging and higher demand marketplaces where buyers were ready and wanting to part with their money.

Absolutely nothing has changed – demand supply – supply demand. When a salon business gives a client what a client is already searching for it's easy to get your appointment book packed.

1980: Health Is The New Punk

This is a little more back-story in detail. I think it's critical to share as I hope you'll see. My mum was a hippy and actually looking back, a radical, in her own way. She used to feed me and my siblings garlic pearl tablets every morning before we all went to school. They stunk to high heaven but apparently made us healthy by clearing our arteries. I don't know why she thought arteries would be blocked at the age of ten.

Mum decided to leave her nursing job and open a health food shop. This was long before health food shops were in fashion especially in the mining town of Leigh, Lancashire where the shop was based. Her first shop was small and infested with mice and rats. It isn't as bad as it sounds because all the shops had infestation but it was manageable infestation (if that makes any sense).

The shop was tiny, maybe just 200 sq. ft. if that. It was old and rotten but had something new going on and something pretty unheard of. It was always packed with people asking advice on their health – AFTER – they had been to see their doctor.

Mum had been a district nurse so she knew a lot about health but wanted to take health in a more organic direction. The people that came to see her clearly loved it to the point that it made good money almost from the start. Marketing wasn't really a thing for mum she just ran the very rare Ad in a local newspaper. She was brillaint at what she did and that was enough to keep her busy. Word of mouth or as we now says ... ATTRACTION!

One day when I was working for my mum a woman came in to ask for advice. As she was speaking to my mother a mouse appeared on a shelf just next to them both but just behind the woman. I could see the mouse and so could my mum. The customer couldn't. The mouse was just doing what mice do in a shop full of grains and rice – eating!

Mum looked at me moving her eyes only in a way she wanted me to do something fast before the lady saw the mouse. I grabbed a box and threw the box over at the mouse. The lady turned to look at me, the box had landed on the mouse, I made a weird excuse and mum had enough time to grab the now unconscious mouse and throw it by the tail behind the counter only to escape and live another day.

The lady bought her vitamins none the wiser and the shop kept on growing until a letter arrived. The letter was from the local council saying they were tearing down the buildings due to age. It wasn't as bad as it sounded. This was mum's perfect opportunity to move into a decent sized shop and grow her business. I was also learning although I didn't realise I was learning about business and getting busy. These were all skills I would take with me into my own salons in the future.

Looking back my mum had a pretty big and radical vision for those years. The most interesting thing looking back was how she branded her new shop up. The only people in those days to really brand up were huge businesses. Local shops had a flat one-dimensional sign that said what they did – that was it!

Mum realised her shop would have to standout because it wasn't quite in the middle of the town as before. She wanted the front loud and it was loud. The shop was renamed to Bee Healthy rather than just The Health Food shop.

Mum created a logo of a tall round yellow and black bumble bee. It had large eyes, long arms, huge round wings and long legs with big black feet. Everything was in strong lines of black and yellow. The font was yellow on black or black on yellow. I loved it I thought it was very cool. I think it was the talk of the town. Loud, outlandish and never to be missed and of course it worked.

Looking back this was another critical business lesson for me in branding and standing out. Yes, mum had the services, the skills and the knowledge but she also had awareness that even in 1980 this wasn't enough. The place had to have a talking point, memory aides on top of amazing services. The shop stood out a mile; you really couldn't miss it on the street.

I loved watching my mum sell. Her customers were usually people unhappy with medical results so they would come to her for something more. Being from a nursing background she would never wait for a customer to ask for anything.

She took a medicinal and observational approach to selling. Under her desk counter was always a blood pressure gauge to find symptoms and also she had a knack of looking at people and knowing what could be wrong.

The person would come into her shop for a bottle of vitamin C and leave the shop with a full bag full of remedies. It's called upselling now. In those days it was called helping people or telling a customer what they needed rather than waiting for the customer to ask! I mean that makes sense right?

If I was helping in the shop it wouldn't be uncommon to be asked to help a customer carry her packed bags of new purchases from the shop over to her car despite the fact they had only come in for advice.

This was an amazing lesson in consulting or listening and observing people as they came into the shop. Mum never believed she was selling anything – yet she knew she had to sell everything – but mostly she listened and advised. She told them what they needed rather than sell them what they wanted. This was to have a huge influence on how I sold in my first salon business.

I realised that you really don't have to sell anything to anyone when they have come to buy what they know they already want. I'd read that again if I were you. This is a realisation in business so powerful yet so simple most will miss it.

My mum didn't have to sell. She found out what they were already looking for and supplied it. This was the backbone of her business and her results showed. My mum always had the best car on the housing estate in fact she had cars when no one owned cars. We were the first family to go abroad for a holiday. We were also one of the first families to buy their own house. The money was clearly coming in for mum and dad.

The new health shop was 2000 sq. ft. It was huge. Once established mum realised people had started to mention to her after they had been to her shop they would go to a café close by for tea. My mum would tell them not to go to cheap cafes as they used non-organic (mum was way ahead of the curve) but they loved going to the café.

So mum being mum made a decision and that was to open a café at the bottom quarter of the shop selling healthy tea and healthy cakes. This was a demand that she saw so she filled the demand after all if they had money and she could sell what they wanted she would do it.

Mum never advertised the café, she never pushed it, and this was simply a demand that people wanted to sit and drink tea after shopping that had now been filled with an organic healthy option.

More lessons again for my future despite that I didn't realise these were lessons. The one thing I would add here is my mum was ahead of the curve. Healthy pies and cakes weren't really a concept in those days so getting her customers to buy them at three times the price of regular pies was never easy yet the café was almost always packed.

The lesson was simple – sell what people want and then when they are ready start selling – **what they want**.

Mum ran her shop for years and expanded in all kinds of areas like sunbeds, fitness equipment, bicycles and more. It was a lesson on business and selling for me that I will never forget.

1989: I'm a Hairdresser
My First Salon

I had gone from gardener to hairdresser.

I'd spent some three plus years as a gardener after leaving school but wanted to use what I felt good at. I'd learnt a lot during my punk haircutting days and was still cutting hair. So I went to college and trained properly.

I hated Hairdressing College it was way too restrictive. For me, it was all about giving people a great haircut and they would pay me for that. College covered zero on how to be great and create great but I kind of understood I had to do it.

I got my first job in a salon in Bolton, and got fired. I was told I was too creative after using slithers of glass to do a haircut! I got my second salon job in Warrington and once again got fired for colouring my hair bright red (unbelievable). I got more jobs and kept getting fired.

Something was telling me something about working for myself so that is what I did.

I had never been short of work since getting fired once again. My phone voice mail (mobile A.D.) when I got home at night was always packed with regular and new clients asking to be booked in. I loved it, I hated it but I was cash loaded. I bought a house, new everything and had money to spend on whatever I wanted. Everything felt good because I was simply filling a demand. The demand really means that the buyer – the client - had already bought their next hairstyle in their head. I just had to show them I had what they wanted to pay for. Once they know of me – they got what they wanted and I got paid.

One day whilst doing a haircut in a client's kitchen the client asked me if I would be interested in opening a shop. Maybe I replied. He showed me a plan, as his shops hadn't been built at this point. He told me I could have the one at the front so passing trade would see it easily. Peter was pretty persuasive to say the least. After the conversation and my unsure response he arrived at my home the same evening with something I had never seen before. It was called a contract. He handed it to me, spent ages once again persuading me and then went away so I could read the contract alone. The contract was a single piece of paper and that paper needed a signature. I didn't read it I just agreed that it sounded cool and I would do it. A shop felt the way forward.

Now I have to tell you at this point I had no idea about putting a salon together and I certainly had never heard a single thing about anything called marketing or promotions. I had been running a short-term mobile hairdressing business purely on demand and had no idea that you had to attract or pull buyers into a brick and mortar business. All I knew was I was making a ton of money and that money had started to be thrown at me.

The shop that was to become my salon had to be built. I went to see the land. It was an old supermarket that had closed and was being rebuilt and divided into eight small units. I did my first staff interview there whilst she and her dad sat on a pile of bricks whilst I sat on a pile of wood. Incredibly she accepted the job and went on to work for me for seven years. Thank you Kerry Dawson.

Once built the shop space was very small at around 250 sq. ft. It was a unit with one glass wall facing into a small mall. My salon was at the front of the mall with my salon door facing the front door where people entered.

The village had a population of just over 3,500 with seven other hair salons. All of the salons had been there over twenty years. One had been there since the very early 1960s. They always hated my salon and me. Honestly I had no time for them I just wanted to succeed.

I never gave any of that business detail a moment of thought. I knew I was a busy high demand hairdresser so I just thought I would be busy in a shop. I had no money to fit out my shop but I did have a decent car. I sold my car for around £5,000 (Ford XR-2) and used the cash to fit my salon out. I managed to fit everything apart from the back room and one sink I couldn't afford to plumb in. Apart from that I was ready to rock 'n' roll!

I opened on May 15th 1989. It was an exciting year for me as my first child was also due. Money was good, I had my own tiny home and now I had a new venture to chase. I'm a salon owner, here we go!

I knew local prices so I simply set my prices roughly the same as everyone else. I can tell you, the price was £6.95 for a ladies cut and blow dry. There's nothing really special about the place apart from I was still listening to punk music so I had punk music blasting whilst most played pop or the Bee Gees!

I believed what most hairdressers believe and it was this.

My skills and being good with my skills would be enough to pack out my salon.

It just wasn't to bring in clients, as you'll see.

On the morning of May 15th I drove down to my salon in the 1972 Mini I had bought for £200 after selling my little sports car to pay for the salon. I parked outside. The mall was brand new; it had no signage and had no promotions before my salon opened.

The first day I walked in on my own ready to take over the world. I had not a single client booked in. The first day I had one lady come in and have a haircut. After eight hours stuck in my new salon I had just £6.95 in the drawer. Deflating!

The next day was the same. And so were the next and the next. The weekend was busy and my old clients were also coming in. Clearly I had a problem very early and I needed to solve the problem otherwise no one would be eating anything!

I thought I had done everything right. Great looking shop, good skills, good services and my prices seemed more than fair. It wasn't good enough and my lack of results began to show very fast.

Even worse ... the reps had discovered my salon and had also found out how naive I was. They call it an easy sell. They told me more stock on display would increase my business. I bought into it. It didn't. My invoices were building fast! I couldn't pay my rent. I started to panic. I knew something had to be done and done fast or I was sunk!

A neighbor I knew that was asking about my new salon and I was telling her my woes told me to write a flyer. I had no idea what a flyer was so I had to find out. She told me it was like this and that and I should write it, print it and then post in the village.

So I walked over to the local printer and he told me it would be 3-4 weeks for the flyer to be printed. This was pretty normal in those days. I asked him what to write and he gave me an example of some flyers. So I went away and wrote a flyer. Four weeks later it came back. I liked it but it was very standard like all salon flyers. Dull. Boring. Not punk rock in the slightest.

The name of my salon went at the top –The Big Scissor Company. A photo of a pretty girl somewhere further down. My salon address and a new client offer of 25% off a £6.95 haircut. Looking back it wasn't great but here's what happened. I was shocked. I also felt inspired.

I walked around my little village on my own with my 3000 flyers. I pushed them through most mailboxes and then went back to my salon. When I arrived on Tuesday to open I got a surprise. The salon voicemail was filled and couldn't take any more messages (It was

a C30 cassette – should have gone C90 ... Google it ;-).
The phone was ringing as I opened the door and suddenly I was busy.

I had just discovered something that I found out is called marketing and it seemed to work. So I did more flyers and kept hand posting them until they seemed to stop working. The flyer was the only marketing or promotion I was doing apart from business cards and letterhead although I hadn't had a clue what I was supposed to do with. All I knew was I was told that a business should have them so I had them. It was standard, letterheads, cards and a flyer or two.

Either way it was all still a struggle and I needed more. Business was now running but not flourishing. Something was missing but I hadn't a clue what to do next.

One day in the brilliant Hairdressing Journal) I saw an advert for Paul Mitchell. The Ad looked like nothing I was seeing anywhere in the hair and beauty industry. I was a long haired guy on a beach with a long hair blonde woman, they were next to a Harley Davidson and the whole look and feel attracted me into the advert. It never really spoke about shampoo or hair product but more about lifestyle. It was rock and roll and it felt like me. I wanted to be part of it.

I thought I could kind of copy this advert and make my salon Ads look similar. I also realised that Paul Mitchell was using different words to anyone else so how could I do that with my words in my flyers or adverts?

At the same time Paul Mitchell offered a seminar in London. This was teaching salon owners like me how to create marketing and get busy but with a twist. It wasn't cheap, I couldn't afford it but I decided to go.

I spent £2,000 on the course and hotel fees and went and had my eyes opened – thank you Paul Mitchell, I stuck with this for around a year or so but honestly being in a club wasn't my thing but it was worth every penny in those days.

This was the first time I realised that words and systems in a salon actually could make a difference in turning my own salon into a business. The words I use in my promotions could, would and did and would make a difference between someone picking up the phone and not picking up the phone.

Not only words but also presentation of the words can increase or decrease my response. Not just presentation of the words but images that surrounded the words. Not only visible image but mental images also. I was amazed not only how it began to change my business but also my whole outlook had suddenly gained confidence and vision!

And then there was a perceptive value. How would the reader of the words and images build their mental perception of my business from what I said in words and presented in image form?

I was reminded Paul Mitchell were doing something cool, and doing something (and still are amazing trailblazers in a me-too industry) that no other company in the salon business had been doing to me and it was this.

They got my attention.

They made me think I was buying a new life and I was in business to build a life not to just open a salon but to create a successful business. My core need was being addressed through Paul Mitchell Ads and that core need was this.

'Alan, you want to have all the good things in life and create a lifestyle that makes you feel good? Selling our stuff in your salon gives you that.'

Get this again: I wasn't building a business I was building a life. The business was simply a tool to build my young life in those days.

My needs were – my life – not just my salon!

This got me thinking.

Clients have choice in the village where my salon was. Do they really want to buy a haircut that all of the salons were selling (cut and blow) or do they want to buy a happier life through looking good? Looking good might get them the perfect partner. Looking good made them feel sexy, gorgeous; handsome every morning they faced a mirror. Looking and feeling good increased the way the performed on a daily basis.

You know it. You know and have seen the step or bounce in people AFTER they leave your salon with a new look. It's an amazing feeling for the client but an even more amazing feeling for use the hairdressers.

A woman or a man who's partner had ran away wanted new partners to see them as sexy and they wanted to feel loved, adored, sexy, special and wanted once again. They knew a new look would help with their confidence, their behaviour, the way they walked and the way they held themselves. In the morning they could look in a mirror and see themselves as this new person rather than the old person that was left abandoned.

In other words hair had become part of her inner resurrection to a new life or becoming a new man or woman once again. Just cool right! Now you might know this but at that time in 1989 I certainly didn't. It changed everything for me.

The client's needs had to be addressed just like my needs were addressed through the brilliant Paul Mitchell Ads. I wanted a lifestyle and that meant a successful business.

She or he wanted a new partner in his or her life and that meant a new sexy, dramatic, cool, and seductive look though a haircut. I could do that!

So rather than my Ads and flyer spelling out the name of my salon, address and what my salon does they now started to take a new shape and approach.

Before I tell you the shape I need you to understand the mental process of the client. Don't forget the Advert now has nothing to do with haircuts and everything to do with your business and your business becoming more successful though filling the real needs of your buyers (I want to feel good about life).

I went through (and still go through) a process of how a client would feel about himself or herself.

Let's imagine this is a woman we are talking about for this example.

I imagined I could see the client feeling fed-up, depressed and sad. I would see her waking up or in the middle of the day. I would see her walking to the mirror in the bathroom with average lighting. I could see her looking into the mirror at the creases around her eyes, her stressed out hollowing skin and her hair looking a mess. She felt older and past it. And then I would see her thoughts and knew she would be saying to herself.

"When's the last time I changed my hair?"

She was asking herself a question. The question wasn't only related to her hair it was ultimately related to her and how she was looking and feeling deeper inside. She understands that a change of look can change everything. You know it can, I know it can.

The new hair requires new make-up, new clothes, new perfume and new actions. This would in return make her feel good about herself again. Her confidence wouldn't force a partner to her but would attract the right person into her life.

Her needs were now being fulfilled through a promise that started in the basics of the Ad. This is the approach that I ethically stole from the ideas Paul Mitchell advertising had given me and literally transformed my business almost overnight.

Here is something else interesting I learnt.

Once the core needs of a client are met this can affect salon pricing in a most powerful way. When I started creating adverts that met the core needs I also took a new direction in pricing in my hair salon. When I had created these new 'needs filling' Ads I also decided that this would take a new audience for my services. This new audience would not only have to pay more but would be very happy to pay more for my hairdressing services that would meet their every need.

I went for a decent price increase but I also had to be strong. Doing this made me feel sick but I also knew I had no option. So the salon closed for the weekend on the Saturday. My fee for the client on the Saturday evening at closing in those days was £6.95. Two days later when I opened after the weekend my new prices were set at £18.95. That's a massive increase.

What do you think happened?

Clients loved the service because core needs that cannot be explained were being met. Core needs that can never be discovered over conference room tables or fixation marketing meetings or core needs that the average repeating marketer would never even think of were being met.

Once a core need is met the resistance to your salon prices are as good as dissolved.

Over a two-day – TWO-DAY – period not only had I almost tripled my salon prices and the result was only to make my salon much busier. This was when I realised that price wasn't the issue for my clients my approach was the issue. I didn't have to be the same price as everyone else's salon. I didn't have to do the same as everyone else. I could charge what I liked for haircuts as long as a true value exchange was being created at the same time.

The price of the haircut only reflected the return on their investment. The investment was more than a haircut it was a feeling of elevation, worthiness, sexiness and a deeper feeling of just feeling good about themselves. You cannot buy this kind of feel good stuff so once an amazing hair service is found to deliver and fulfill those feelings; the price now becomes a long secondary option.

And the cool part for your salon...

... I had discovered that when a price is the same as everyone else's price you are giving the buyer the final decision. I realised that a client would phone many salons and make a choice of salon on a personal decision – not price. How could it be price when all prices, all perceptive looks of the sales were almost identical?

Out of seven small salons in the village where my first salon was located all the salons charged around £6.95, as did I when I opened. Now I was the only salon that was charging £18.95. Price alone made me standout in the most dramatic way and this only increased my salon takings - by three times!

I had gone from no confidence in my little struggling salon to incredible confidence and the feeling that I can now take on the world from this very same little salon.

I also discovered this next extremely powerful tool for my salon and the results were astonishing.

As you know, in the hair industry it is pretty traditional that a stylist meets the client once the client is sitting in the chair where they have their haircut. In a lot of cases the client's hair would even be washed before the stylist meets the client especially if the salon is busy. I certainly did this when I started.

But it's always worth remembering a client will arrive into any new salon nervous. This is a natural way for any person to feel when going into any new salon. And then when the client feels at their worst or most vulnerable moment with wet, flat, un-styled hair and possibly eye make-up running after water splashes then meet a new stylist for the first time. Not only are most clients unlikely to open up and talk about their hair but also they are unlikely to spend more money whilst in your salon.

I knew my clients were thinking more than I could know so I wanted to know more about how they were thinking. Once I knew how they were thinking and feeling I could make them an offer to solve their current thoughts and feelings. Once their thoughts and feelings are solved not only does a client relax, they also develop a trust beyond the usual trust. By the way the best way to find out what they are thinking is to simply – ask them!

I thought about different ways to find out the problems and came to the conclusion that the way a Doctor would find out would be to sit face to face, ask searching questions and then offer the perfect solution. Looking back this was also the way mum had built her mini health food empire so this was a good time to put a lesson into practice.

I created a questionnaire on a clipboard just like a doctor would have used (iPad now), I would sit face-to-face with my new clients and then after introducing myself would go through the questions one at a time and tick off the answers. I created the sheets with three layers. White on the top, yellow next and then pink. The client was given a copy of the sheet. This would be an agreement that what was discussed was the clients thoughts and not just the thoughts of a hairdresser. Clients were blown away with this little routine but I was always nervous doing it.

Once the sheet was filled out after 20-minues of consulting I would then offer the solution. Now remember this. The client had arrived for a £18.95 haircut. After a consultation like this they understood their hair problems were more than a haircut. I understood to get the desired results it would take a little more. This would result in a recommendation or advice or myself. For example if the client needed more volume a color could give her more volume and texture. If she needed her hair to look thicker I would advise the client use certain products on her hair at home and so on.

Once the overall solution was recommended and the service was carried through the client would have another fear and it was this...

"How am I going to manage my hair at home?"

I realised this and would spend extra time showing the client how to manage her hair at home with new products and styling tools. Now here is the thing.

My invoices at the checkout went from £18.95 to as high as £200 on many occasions (this was 1989/90).

This whole process led me into a different hairdressing path. It had no longer become about survival hairdressing but had now become about value exchange hairdressing. I was hungry to be successful and despite the problems early on I also had the drive and energy to overcome anything.

I hadn't sold out. This was still punk rock. I was still breaking the rules. I had become the anti-salon in my area. I was the Jonny Rotten of the local salon trade and the local salons really didn't like what I was doing.

They told everyone I was a rip off whilst clients told everyone I was the best thing going!

This newly discovered business process got me thinking about something else that I mastered in my second salon. It's worth mentioning now because like everything so far it also applies to your business.

I realised that every client goes through a process or path of the mind before a process of buying. It can start at any point and can be started by events of life or just the thirst to change or put things right in their mind through change. When I say change I of course mean a change of hair.

Going back to the woman or man looking in the mirror most of the times they don't really notice their hair. Then one day they might see an image and that image is repeated into their mind time and time again. That image is a hairstyle that they don't have but love the idea of having.

They then start to look at their own hair in the mirror and even start to ask others if that hairstyle would suit them. Once others agree (or disagree) the thought process of change has really started.

From the thoughts and initial hair images seen by the client the process is taken to another level. That level involves collecting pictures and ideas for their new hairstyle. The images can be collected on their phones and once again shown to friends for their opinion. Eventually the client – lets just says a woman for now – decides to go into a salon and have her hairstyle changed.

At this stage the resistance to paying for a new hairstyle has gone. In their mind they have already paid for and bought the new hairstyle.

Before they get to the salon they go through a salon or stylist search process. They think about their current salon and might reason that they have already been going for three years and no offer of change has been made so the trust isn't there for a redesign. You are seen as someone that trims their hair – that's it!

They then search for a salon and stylist they can trust without risk. This is done through asking friends first, searching online and looking at ratings online. In my day it was simply a case of asking others.

Once the salon for the new style has been decided the client will either make contact with the salon or walk into the salon. They haven't bought into the salon just yet but they will decide based on reaction they get from the salon staff on the visit.

This can be how the phone call is handled to how the staff reacts as she walks in. At this point a client can still be lost. If lost – cash is lost. I couldn't afford to lose clients like that can you?

So once I worked out this mental process with clients I then started to test different things on the phone. If a client rang and said I would like to know the price of a restyle in your salon most salons would then hand over the price list.

If they phoned my salon I had created and tested script that would convert or get appointments booked. The script had to be carried out by all of my staff.

Here's an example of the script for you. Just so you know I would call all of the local salons and further beyond to find out exactly how they reacted on the phone.

Other salon:

'Hi can you tell me the price of a cut and restyle please?'

'Yes from £25.50 up to £45.50'

'OK thank you.'

'OK thank you.'

Any salon I rang appeared to have given no thought about the mental process new clients go through or even trying to book the new enquiry in. I still think most salons even today still don't understand this process or give it any real thought.

I had worked out and I knew the mental journey clients were going through so I picked up the phone this way.

My salon:

"Hi can you give me the price of a cut and restyle please?'

'Hi this is Alan speaking. I am happy you called us because we are hair redesign specialists. This means that when you come into our salon a restyle specialist will sit with you and go through every issue you have with your hair right now, suggest at least six different restyles you can have, give you free advise on how to look after your new restyle and even show you all the products and tools you will need for your new hairstyle when you get home. David is free on Saturday at 2:00pm shall I book you in then?'

Something magical had taken place and it was this.

Price was never the issue when the client called. She simply called to break the ice and see if this salon could help her. Also, all of her fears and objections had been covered so she was happy to book in with David at 2:00 pm.

Finally, we rarely mentioned the price over the phone but we would give an estimate if asked again. The reason again is I now understood that price wasn't the issue – value exchange was. This was another discovery that was to transform my new salon business.

And as you can see and will understand the journey of any salon client coming into your salon doesn't change and cannot change. The process of booking a haircut buying isn't a process of persuading it is a process of fulfillment of basic human needs such as the need to look and feel good again. The needs are what persuade the client to book an appointment not the convincing words or the endless barrage of direct attempts to force her to book an appointment. Or in lots of cases when I have worked with and tested salon phone answering - as little effort as possible!

The basic human need was the client wanted to feel safe, feel good, feel sexy, feel wanted and have a euphoric feeling of her becoming alive after her new look.

And believe me after working in the hairdressing business since 1982 there really is no such thing as six weeks between good and bad hair. Bad hair can destroy a woman's life for much longer than six weeks. So the process of choice of salon for a new haircut is detailed and as precise as it can be. You know this stuff!

The need always has to be and must be a good value exchange after all anyone could do a haircut but not anyone could offer the twists and turns I was adding into my new business and all with no extra budget being spent to do this and of course no social media at the time.

Don't get me wrong not everything was good, I had problems of every size but I also took time to try and work out what needed doing to make things happen. It really didn't take me long to realise that a salon just doesn't get busy by sitting and waiting for clients to walk through the door. It really doesn't happen like that.

Getting clients through the door takes effort and constant effort at that. It also takes an ongoing plan of action. A one off hit running a single ad was never going to make anything happen.

In the early days of my salon it was it was just me, my junior Kerry and eventually another stylist who worked just two days a week. When Sue worked in the salon we just never had enough space. In total there were just five chairs in this salon with two sinks but only one sink had been plumbed in properly. It could get seriously chaotic.

Even in this salon I experimented and changed things. Not everything worked all the time. For example I had a large black ash desk for reception. It was actually a 2nd hand office desk but kind of did the job. It was too big through and was stealing a lot of space. I eventually got rid of the desk so I could add retail into the window but also try to add one more seat, which frankly was as good as impossible.

And although the salon was at the front of a small mall of eight shops the mall was very quiet and unless you actually walked into the mall the salon really couldn't be seen. So the small start didn't hold me back and in fact gave me a testing ground to build my bigger salon.

I did learn this powerful lesson and it was this.

If it isn't working make the changes as fast as humanely possible. If I waiting for others to make those changes they could spend months doing something I could fix in a day or so.

I discovered there are many things that can kill my salon – like staff not wanting to do more than they can get away with but I also realised they only got away with that because I was allowing them and not being clear enough on what I wanted for my business.

I realised that many of those that say they want to help me build my business really just wanted to sell me more of their product. I then had to sell that product or it would simply build up more debt. I also knew for sure it was up to me to learn how to sell the product.

I also learned that waiting for a client to walk through the door was a fool's game. Yes clients will walk through the door but it was always faster if I did everything in my power to pull them into my salon faster rather than sit and wait.

Ultimately, with my first salon I accepted that I am the one responsible for my salon business being a success or being a failure. There are always things I could do but I had to learn to take action to make my salon business work and happen as fast as possible.

Everything was always a choice but I had to learn how to make the right choices and then take action to make sure those choices actually work. With all of the action, choices and progress I had made I finally started pulling clients in but I really wanted to increase the momentum by huge amounts. I now also wanted and needed to be a much bigger salon. I wanted the number one salon position.

Around one year into my first salon it was clear that the premises were far too small. I literally had clients falling out of the front door. On weekends I had even put two benches outside the salon for waiting clients to sit on as we worked through a relentless torrent of clients from 8am to 5:30pm with no stops or breaks. It was crazy but amazing!

At this stage I was using just one or two flyers that I had created and a regular slot on the local weekly newspaper. Being a village environment it felt easier to build up a base of clients very quickly.

This is where I realised that loyalty to one salon although spoken about and thought about as a gospel, it didn't really exist. Clients despite going to one salon for say ten years or more would happily if not nervously swap salons as long as the feedback from others was good and of course the work was good also.

I had taken no real notice of the power of referrals or clients coming back for more. I simply arrived at the shop, opened the doors and worked like a happy slave from morning until night.

And by the way ... I was making a serious attempt at doing things as different as I could. I played punk music very loud, looked the part, did a lot of crazy stuff in the salon and felt like I was creating an environment that once visited the clients wouldn't forget. It was working and working like crazy.

However, the salon at just 250 sq. ft. was far too small.

1990: More Space Bigger Salon More Problems

I needed, I wanted a much bigger salon and wanted it fast. At the same time my mum wanted out of her big health food shop premises. It was 2000 sq. ft. and her landlord kept pushing up the rent almost year on year. He was a real creep. I was about to have the same creepy guy as my landlord.

I think looking back mum missed a perfect opportunity to build a nice little empire. She had built a really great brand and her place was packed with buyers looking for cures for health issues every minute of everyday. One of the earliest chains of health stores wanted to buy her out. They had the cash and the investment to grow. Mum was more of a do it all yourself business owner and didn't have the cash to take her business to another level. She should have sold. She didn't, she simply wrapped up everything and handed the lease over to me after all the new agreements were put into place.

I learned a lot from mum's health food store but now I had to keep my newer, bigger salon packed, stay focused, build a real business, make things work, stay busy and get my salon growing and changing as fast as I could. Mum had now gone into a new sunbed business and I was about to hit a ton of new problems with my new salon. This really meant I would have to learn faster than ever before.

I might sound like I knew what I was doing but I really didn't. It was always chaotic in the background but a planned chaos. I signed a new lease for 15-years. This was a big mistake. I should have bought the place as I was offered the premises for sale.

Anyway now I was signed in, I had a new landlord and I had to convince my clients that went to my small salon five miles away to drive from the village to this town.

Of course there was a fit out of the salon and it was a huge place. I had around twenty chairs downstairs, four backwashes a large staff room, huge reception area, massive retail area and something I really wanted which was a big waiting area in the salon. Then of course I had to get all the usual stuff on loans, deals etc. I felt at my limit in cash and expense so this salon had to work. It was also costing me money from the day I signed so the clock was ticking.

Everything I had learnt from my small 250 sq. ft. salon over the past 18-months now had to be ramped up before the new 2000 sq. ft. salon opened and time was feeling very short.

This town was a very different scenario from my village salon location. The population was around 125,000. In the town center I also had strong competition of around 35 salons. Some had been in the town for just a few years. Other salons had been there 30-plus years and many others well over 20-years.

If my new salon was going to work it would take every bit of creative juice and previous experience I had.

Here we go!

I knew the earlier I started to push the salon the bigger the impact would be. I had no open date but that tended up being irrelevant as the builder was a waste of time and always behind on everything.

I had used and liked the marketing model for promoting movies. I loved how they spent months doing teasers and trailers and posters. I always wanted to watch the fast approaching movie and I thought if it works for them surely it'd work for me?

So I decided to copy the movie launch model with strong posters and run a simple campaign in the local newspapers to be supported by the posters on the exterior of the building as the salon was being fitted out and remodeled.

I can't quite remember the Ads but they went very like this.

A new kind of hairdresser is coming (making a claim of NEW in a town packed with salons)

A salon with a real difference (We are not the same as the other 35 salons we do things different here)

Quality hairdressing from quality hairdressers (we are quality – they are not because if they were they would be saying the same)

Premium hairdressing services from hairdressing experts (this is a premium service – we are the best – the others are average)

The ultimate hairdressing service (The use of the word is definitive and the use of the word premium makes a statement of being the best)

And so on. It all sounds very well thought out then – the truth is it wasn't. This was all stuff I had read and studied on other adverts like Paul Mitchell or movie posters I liked and simply thought read cool and had pulled me in. I just felt if the ads worked for them and convinced me it would work on my clients.

Another thing in those days; I had also thought a lot about cars in those days. It was my age of course but there were a few things cars did that got my interest.

I always wanted a BMW and almost dreamt about BMW in those days. I knew they were the best. I agreed they were the ultimate driving machine as their adverts say. I knew they were the most expensive for me. I knew they had German engineering and I wanted one as fast as I could get one.

But here's the thing.

I had never driven one, been in one or even touched one. All I knew was I wanted one.

Why?

BMW had done an incredible job at building what I will call a perceptive positioning and it was brilliant. It had worked on me and millions of others and I realised early in my salon business if it feels like the right thing to do I just do it ... especially if someone else has done it and proved it works!

So I decided to create a secondary marketing campaign modeled on BMW and create a perceptive positioning campaign for this new salon. This simply meant that my choice of words had to create the impression that this new salon was going to be not just good but the very best out of the 35 salons in this town. It had to go ever further. Like BMW had created a belief in me that if I wanted to drive the very best it had to be a BMW I wanted the same perception in my salon, which would be if you want the very best hairdressing you had to go to my salon.

Re-read the paragraph above until you really get it. This is probably the most powerful paragraph in this whole book.

I created a list of words I wanted to use alongside the commonly thought about hairdressing words, simplified everything yet focused on the power each word would have.

BMW had been using The Ultimate Driving Machine so I decided to use The Ultimate Quality Hairdressing Salon.

Outside on my signage I decided to use the words in huge 3D ... QUALITY HAIRDRESSING. For me I had taken a punk rock stand against the 35-salons in the town and screamed out loud that my salon specialized in quality. The power of that one single word when sat next to the word hairdressing was huge for my business.

I had the posters I mentioned above created and I carefully dripped out a campaign letting the passer-by know that not just another hairdressing salon was opening but a quality hairdressing salon that would deliver the ultimate hairdressing services.

When I say dripped out again this was based around a movie style campaign I learnt very quickly that a marketing campaign isn't simply a one-off event because I learnt through experience that people forget very quickly. This had to be repeated time and time again into the community to let people know this was coming and would be here to stay once the salon arrived. I always booked my campaigns well in advance and always book 12-weeks at a time rather than just a one-off shot.

So the new salon was now in motion (slow motion that was). My old salon was just 250 sq. ft. This was a whole new level at 2000 sq. ft. and it was up to me to make sure it was packed from morning till night.

We didn't use the upstairs right away so the working space when I first opened was 1000 sq. ft.

What I want to share with you is this because it was a total shock for me and it was also everything I never expected at the time.

A bigger salon can open up a whole new can of worms and massive problems.

Before in my smaller salon my staff was good, business was good, and profits were good in fact it was all really more than great.

Once I moved I could never have known it but I was about to face a whole new set of problems I could never have even imagined. Including a demand for almost £20,000 from the Inland Revenue that had to be paid there and then and of course the inevitable staff walk out on mass that left ME as the only member of staff in a huge salon and a collapsed ceiling and huge flood that filled the whole salon on the day of opening!

1991: The Big Salon

I was now about to go from 1.5 staff to 16 staff.

I was upsizing from 250 sq. to 2000 sq. ft.

I was moving from a tiny village of 3000 to a small town of 125,000.

My rent was about to increase 6x.

I thought I knew everything about running a hairdressing salon but I really knew a little.

The lease was now signed. The salon was due to open in the autumn. I had taken out a huge loan to fit out this salon but had also decided I would do as much as I could do myself. The schedule was now running very late and I was paying for everything despite not being open yet. It was costing me before we opened and debt was rising.

The builder was hopeless, and turned up when he wanted to turn up. Just the usual stuff I suppose but then I just wasn't used to it. I thought everyone would show the same respect for others I had been used to showing. Clearly now and this was to teach me some even bigger lessons very soon. My advice is never asking a friend to fit your shop. This was a friend. After the fit out we never spoke again.

The adverts had been telling everyone that the salon was about to open now for months. The huge window posters had also been saying the same things with words that sounded almost religious as in ... THE SECOND COMING ... but of course it wasn't Jesus it was just me.

So as you can understand the local salons wanted to know who was arriving, as did the local population. The buildup was pretty huge.

My new salon was also five miles away from my other small salon. I didn't want to keep both at this stage I wanted to be super focused on one. I sold the small one to a friend and allowed them to pay me off gradually.

I know people dream of two or three or more salons but my own reality was I really never gave it much thought. I simply thought the money selling the small salon would cover some of the bills in the new place. I also very naively thought all my staff and all of my clients would travel the five miles into the town. They didn't.

So in actual fact this was like starting all over again. I could probably count on both hands the clients that were willing to travel from a village into a town. Of course the hardcore clients I had been servicing for years still came but it wasn't enough to pack out my new salon. Also the impression is stylist will bring a ton of clients with them. That's a myth most of the time.

Finally, after blood, sweat and tears the big salon opened. I had problems on opening day. One being about half an hour after the shop opened with my brand new team of six, the ceiling caved in over the backwashes and the salon was flooded from end to end.

This was a bad start – an omen maybe – but a bad start all the same. Business was incredibly slow. After just a few weeks some staff just moved on due to no clients for them and I had to let staff go leaving myself and just two stylists and one junior to try and make this new huge salon work.

We would all arrive at the salon. I was starting to dread the drive to the place, as I knew when we all arrived there would be no clients in. It was a case of all of my staff sitting in the back room and just waiting for the call to come out and see a client. The problem with that was the longer they had nothing to do the less they wanted to do when clients arrived. Staffing problems just escalated and escalated fast.

This was, this is salon life. Staff issues, unpaid invoices, unpaid rates, delays in rent and all of the usual major problems that I see also common today.

It was heartbreaking but the pressure constantly forced me to find solutions. I read more, found out more and spoke to more people for advice on how to get this salon packed and packed as fast as possible.

And we had other problems like the local rats!

One day one of the juniors went up the stairs where most of the time the light bulb was dead. The room was pretty dark, as it had no windows. Each day the junior had to simply open the tumble dryer door to leave any towels in to breathe and dry for the next morning. One morning just after we opened the junior walked up the open stairs to get the towels. Suddenly we heard a loud scream and as she ran downstairs she tripped over a towel, did a single summersault, landed upside down with her legs in the air and was knocked unconscious.

A large rat had run off from out of the warm towels only to live another day. This was a recurring problem but never stopped us doing great hairdressing.

After six months of teething major and problems I was breaking every rule you can think of in my salon. We were doing stuff not a lot of other salons were doing at the time. Breakfast clubs, movie nights, restyle evenings, sample programs, style check services, new services, invented services and frankly a lot of made up or renamed services that sound very different to what other salons were doing.

My rule was very simple; if other salons were doing it we should do the very opposite and that approach was working.

Even on prices I had prices in this salon that were way beyond what anyone could charge in this town. It gave us a powerful perception as the best option for hairdressing.

I knew if we were the same price we would be seen as a choice. I had most of my prices double and in some cases triple the local prices of the other 35 salons. This gave us a strong position in the town. Of course the quality of the work has to support the higher prices.

Remember I said my mother was a health freak with her own health shops. So we had books lying around and besides henna I realised other things could colour hair and of course cut hair.

So I started coloring hair and cutting hair with things like Rhubarb, curry powders, beetroot and more. As far as cutting went I would cut hair with glass, long hair with clippers and just about anything else that was breaking some lines and boundaries at the time in our little town.

But I wanted number one.

I wanted to be the No.1 salon and number 2. Just wouldn't do it.

In the town I also had problems from other salons. They would do things like endlessly book fake appointments all the time, glue up my door locks and other weird things.

One day I had a stylist come to me for a job. After an interview I discovered he was working at one of the main competition. I offered him the job. He was a nice guy but never stopped asking me questions. I had no experience so I simply told him what he kept asking.

Around five weeks into his job he just didn't turn up for work in the salon. I left it one day and tried to call his house (before mobiles) but with no luck. After doing a little detective work one of the other staff told me he was working back at his old salon that was literally just up the road. Even more unbelievable was the story that was to follow. The other salon had paid him more cash to work for me so he could report back everything about my salon to his other boss. Once he found out all he could he simply went back to his 'real' job' and reported everything about as many internal workings of my salon as possible to his old and now again current boss. I was angry but flattered at the same time.

And of course a few other things I won't give energy to here.

I think the other salons loved to hate my salon because I was the salon that eventually they had to run behind despite them being established for over 30-years! I had invented new services, had a huge retail area (no one had this then), I was doing so much boots-on-the-ground guerilla marketing you just wouldn't believe it.

It was very hard work but I had kids to feed, I had bills to pay I had a lot of money going out every week and every month. I had to make this salon not just work but I wanted the very best!

I knew this.

To be No.1 we had to offer the best hairdressing, the best colorists, the best service, the best products and just about the best of everything.

So we trained, we discovered, we learnt and under my direction we did our own thing. I stayed single focused and pushed forward hard everywhere I could.

As you can see we eventually got very busy but it wasn't easy and that process involved a lot of trying things out.

Each day I had a list of things to do to make sure the salon and the staff was kept busy. This is the times before the web. No email, no Facebook, no anything yet I still had my morning list. The list involved at least 15-20 things that had to be done before anything else was done. I had one rule on my mind that has never changed.

What brings money into the salon is what gets done first. That means other things still got done but it wasn't a priority to clean the salon or change the magazines as a first job. Yes that stuff keeps the salon in shape but it isn't what I call a prime cash driver.

I called it my stack list. I still call it the stack even today when working with salons and other businesses.

The stack looked a little like this.

- A-boards out
- Flyers stacked and measured
- Stylist promotions who and when
- Car park board out
- Shopping center board out
- Window signs clear
- Flyer holders and tables outside the shop
- Info packs ready to go
- Stand-by list created
- Staff organized to hand out flyers
- Daily goals for staff
- Goals for the salon
- Manage the daily diary
- Manage the columns
- Referral program double checked and in place

And so on. The list was maybe around 20 items long and critical to the start of each day. All on the list had to be done. This would take around 15-30 minutes top!

For example I worked this out. If we gave out 20 flyers or vouchers on the street I could expect at least one back. So to gain 20 new clients I also knew I had to hand out at least 400 flyers. That rule has never changed.

I would allocate say 500 flyers to be handed out daily! It was critical for me that I knew that actual number.

If I advertised in the newspaper I learnt to never expect a rush of clients.

And I also knew that if I ran one advert for one week the effect was as good as zero.

I learned that the most effective adverts would run for as long as 12-weeks. So after 12-weeks I could see the effect of running the local ads in the newspaper. In fact I had one advert that I ran time and time again in the newspaper. That advert never changed. It broke every rule that salons use when advertising. It even had no pictures yet was the most successful advert I ever ran.

That same advert is used today in my client's salons. One salon owner reported to me that that advert had taken around £74,000 in increased sales through his salon.

And of course the endless direct mail or letters.

I bought a computer in 1992. I saw the potential but had no idea how to use it if I'm honest so I put it in my wardrobe and left it there for a few years. Then around 1995-I think) a system came out that literally myself and another salon in the UK owned. This gave me the ability to send letters to my clients.

Every Monday for years I would spend a full day printing out very slowly around 500 letters. This was the day it would take a couple of minutes to print a single A4 letter. Then on Tuesday I would actually still have to lick every stamp, hand write on every envelope and then take to the post office the letters in large black bin liners. The effort was massive and hard work. The results were extra ordinary. The salon was packed morning till night every single day of the week with NO discounts, high prices but crazy persuasive and internal salon offerings that only ever got seen by my clients.

At this stage my prices were as much as three times higher than most of my competitors and it was just nuts in the salon. Price was never an issue.

I kept running direct mail every single week from the week I started right up until the last week in my salon in 2003.

Then of course the web arrived. I decided to collect email addresses after building my own salon website. I thought it would be better to email and cheaper. The problem was in 1997 when I started asking for email addresses not many people had one and those that did didn't want to share in those days. I think a lot of people then never really thought email would catch on.

So there were these things and more. The point really was I never sat and waited for clients to walk through the door. I learned and understood that the more I did the more a return I would get. I could never accept failure and did my best to solve every problem thrown at me. They can all be solved that's for sure.

Just about everything the local salons didn't do... I did and that is partly to blame for my salon going from a start-up to its No.1 position in that town.

I was still learning though and still had to take the bad with the good.

I was and probably still am a sucker for a good salesman. I got behind on my invoices in a big way.

One day two huge guys walked into my salon. The salon was packed. That meant there could be anything from twenty clients in there at one time. The reception area was packed with maybe eight clients sitting and waiting.

And then these two bullies in cheap suits asked for me - Alan... I heard them and I walked over to the front desk. They loudly explained for all to hear they were from the Inland Revenue and demand I pay £18,000 there and then. I couldn't, I didn't and everyone could hear every word being spoken. They then told me in a loud manner that if I look out the salon window I could see a large van across the street. They then explained that if they do not leave with a payment they would take the equipment from the salon. You could still do this in those days.

Everyone in the salon heard everything. It was an embarrassment to say the least especially as the salon appeared to be doing so well! It was but my financial management was terrible.

I asked them to go upstairs to the private area and they agreed but didn't want to because they had more power in front of the clients. We went upstairs and I only just manage to squeeze my way out of this situation by talking and giving them what were known as post-dated checks to be cashed at certain dates. That disaster was avoided.

Also my gullibility for retail became a problem for me. Looking back I couldn't say no to reps in those early days and they knew it. I would sign up for deals that truthfully were decent deals but my reality was I couldn't pay the bills when they arrived, as they were huge. As time went on I managed to get a grip of everything.

This of course is salon life. I had those salons for a long time and faced every single issue imaginable. Yes there were times when I couldn't pay wages, I couldn't pay my rent or I couldn't even pay myself.

Yes I had huge staff walkouts, staff stealing, staff being poached and staff that were lazy.

And of yes after employing hundreds of staff over that time I thought I'd seen everything until something else took place that would shock me once again.

One day one of my juniors I trained from school and was now a stylist for the past five years told me it was time to move on. I loved her in the salon but it was good for her. She told me she was moving away to live with her sister in another city and would get a job there. I appreciated her honesty and wanted to give her a good send off. I bought her scissors for £500; chocolates, cards and we all sent her off.

The following week I opened the local newspaper to see this same girl that worked for me for years had half page advert saying she was now at this other salon that was literally 500 feet from my salon. I am smiling as I write this but I wanted to kill her at the time. This is salon life right?

Yet the reality was this.

I had built a mini empire that had even built me a large five bedroomed house, given my 2-3 holidays away every year and supported my family and life. It was amazing.

I had even stolen the No.1 slot for the best hairdressing salon in that town of 35-salons. Anyone could have had that slot but I was the one that went for it.

I had created a salon that was perceived to be the very best at everything we were doing. My prices were the highest. My staff was the busiest. My marketing systems were just over-the-top and I was even able to build my own huge house in the process.

It could be brutal.

It could be kind.

This was my salon business.

YET … the most brutal thing that happened to me whilst having my salon is a story I really don't tell that much. In fact I haven't really told it to anyone since it happened in 2003. Not that I never got over it I did and have but it was a brutal end to 17-years of a really successful salon.

I'll share it with you now. It's a fitting close to this salon experience story and pretty dramatic.

Towards the end of 2002 I had found a buyer for my big salon, as I wanted to get out of the business of owning and running a salon. I had been in this shop for 17-years of lease and really wanted new direction. I had accidently started a consulting and marketing business that was just crazy busy on the back of my salon work so that was where I was heading for now.

Finally, I found two guys to buy my salon and they had cash and were ready to roll. They would have taken the salon there and then and even brought all of the cash when we initially met in a carrier bag but I had a lease issue.

Once I told the landlord I was selling I also had the issue that the lease was also about to end. The landlord knew I was selling so he felt part of the sale price should be his. He refused to renew a lease to me unless I gave him the quarter of the sale value in cash. He told me blunt, 'give me the cash or I won't renew the lease'. If I didn't have the lease how could I now sell my business?

Selling the salon at this stage was secret because as I knew staff simply go if they feel the salon is about to close or be sold. Because I was now in a small war with the landlord, he had started to come into the salon and threaten to tell all of my staff my plans. Finally, one day when I wasn't in the salon and we had been fighting for six-months about this lease and my refusing to hand him the cash he arrived at the salon and announced to everyone that the salon was closing as the lease was about to expire and I wouldn't renew with him.

At 11:30am that morning I had a call to tell me that I had a full staff walkout and instant resignation. I also had buyer that had the cash but now didn't want to buy for obvious reasons. I didn't realise but the landlord had also spoken privately to the new buyers and told them he would let them have the shop for the quarter of the sale price rather than the much larger amount that had been agreed. It was a no brainer for the new owners and why not. I had no staff. I closed the doors and simply walked away. Two weeks later the new boys had a salon that had been there for 17-years handed on a plate and of course employed my old staff.

I don't blame them in the slightest after all if I could get a fully operational, running and very busy salon for a fraction of the price I would go for it also. It hurt like hell and frankly I cried that day and many days after.

The only thing I had left to sell from that salon was stock, my database and the actual salon phone number, which I sold for just a tiny amount to a salon just down the road! Total amount I walked away with was around under £500 after 17-years of huge success.

Broken? Not really everything had its time and purpose and this was one of those moments for me.

But ...

The lessons in the hairdressing business, in business and in life were huge. Rather than looking back at the loss I also felt as time passed so after many doors were now ready to be opened for me and I was free to pursue new things.

And also the takeover and the way it happened did hurt but it also made me realise after 17-years this was a tiny blip during what had been a totally spectacular run in a small town where even I had wiped out one or two established salons with my new mad crazy packed out hairdressing business over this 17-year period. I had even turned over millions in cash through my salon desks during this period. How could I have been sad when I should have really been nothing but grateful for a 17-year life changing experience that gave me the most wonderful life?

I wish I could tell you everything on these pages but the book would be far too big. I just want you to know that being a salon owner is almost the same for everyone.

Its just problems that need solutions – that really is it!

Those that solve the problems are those that find the solutions and take action are the winners in our business.

Nothing ever fixes itself.

I loved the salon business. I loved my salons. I loved the people.

1989 – 2003:
The Big Salon Lessons

So from 1989 to 2003 what did I really learn from having three salons, employing hundreds of stylists and juniors, and dealing with every aspect of running a salon?

A lot of what I never expected but the hard work pays off. When I say hard work I really do mean blood sweat and tears, being awake all night, feeling stressed and under pressure, working 7-days a week and 24-hours some days. Yes, it really was hard work but worth every ounce of energy and huge rewards.

I found out I had to know what I wanted from my salon because if I didn't know how would my staff know?

I realised that I had to be a strong leader. If I didn't lead my salon and team they would do whatever they wanted, when they wanted and how they wanted.

I quickly found out that if I got too close to my staff they would treat me as a fellow stylist and show no respect for my decisions as the salon owner.

I soon found out that if I simply walked in every day and expected the salon to work and be going anywhere was delusional. I had to direct the salon at all times.

I found out that appointing a manager just because they had been there the longest was a big mistake. Managers have to be appointed on merit but more important have the management skills in place.

I realised that the only way I could ever get off the shop floor was to have as many tested systems in place as possible. This also included a manager that had been not only trained by myself but was accountable to myself daily.

I found out most staff are great but some staff are a pain in the ass and should simply be removed. It took me years to realise staff had to be in line with my bigger vision and outcome.

I realised that young staff have the passion and drive older staff can lose. This should always be nurtured and pushed forward. The really are the future.

I discovered that being a really good hairdresser was never enough once I had a salon. You can do and take all the training you like but it just isn't enough to create a real salon business.

I found out that being the same is just ... the same! Taking the opposite direction to all of the local salons helped me to build a very successful salon business.

I learned trust isn't something you give to everyone it has to be earned. I quickly learned who I couldn't trust but really never learnt who I could trust 100% in the business apart from myself.

I also learned everyone that is your friend usually aren't your friends. Staff can love you for 10-years and hate you in a day!

The only way to get my salon packed was to TELL EVERYONE we were really good hairdressers. The assumption that the public would just know is a stupid assumption and bad business advice. I discovered not only do people not know but also nobody really cares unless you tell him or her what and who you are.

With that in mind I had so many materials written around the salon where clients could pick them up and read about my salon, my team and my services. I put simple A4 sheets into simple folders and the clients loved them. They would sit, open the folders up and read what we were up to. Anywhere a client would sit in the salon I would also have signs. Signs everywhere of every size telling the clients continually how great we were or what we were up to in the salon. I did the very same in adverts. I rarely used adverts for offers but always focused on telling the public that we were number one.

I learned that you have to continually also tell the public, assure the public, show off to the public and use as many ways possible to get the public's attention. This was the only to ensure the salon was always busy.

If I had an opportunity to get out of the salon and onto the streets I would take it with my staff. I rarely waited for the public to find us – we simply went where the public were and shared our great hairdressing with them.

I also learnt that marketing wasn't a one off event. It isn't one of those things that you decide to do like maybe run and advert because things are a little slow. I learned that advertising as like paying the wages it had to be done every single week with no breaks. I discovered that if I had a break in my marketing this would also mean a break in my profits. I did what I could do daily.

I used everything I could use at the time, as we had no Internet. I started using direct mail in 1992 and used to do it myself. I used it to send reminders, celebrations and more. The time it could take was crazy but the returns were huge. I would write and mail out around 500 letters every Tuesday morning. I still love sending real letters today because no one really uses them anymore.

I discovered the power of a handout or flyer. These things were so powerful that they could take a slow day and turn it into a crazy day and that is no exaggeration. It was always very simple, we just stood outside the shop and simply hand the flyers out. There was never a day or a week where the flyers never went out.

I discovered if I wanted a busy business and thriving salon this was always going to take a lot of extra effort.

I also discovered that my service had to match any claims I was making. I once heavily promoted an experienced senior stylist as the greatest thing ever based on her qualifications and what she told me. The problem was – she wasn't! It backfired.

I discovered that whatever I was saying I had to be telling the absolute truth at all times and that includes selling my staff.

And yes I discovered a lot about people and staff. Let me say right at the start I had some incredible staff. I can't recall but at the time I loved them working with me and sharing their skills and efforts.

I discovered they can and will leave for some of the most outrageous reasons. I learnt that staff rarely stays because of the money; there is always more to the story.

I also discovered how easy staff can lie to my face and tell me they were getting a new job in a new town with a new salon only to see a large advert for their services in the local newspaper announcing they were now working for my mortal hairdressing enemy on the opposite side of the street.

And finally I discovered in time that staff are just people and are just human beings like myself.

They did what they did for good and bad because that is what I allowed at the time. They like myself are simply in search of a better life through their job so if I am not helping them to find that better life it was usually because what I provided through my job for them simply didn't deliver.

And of course – some of them are just little shits ... lets never forget that! And yet another discovery working with salons today compared to yesterday is this.

Clients basic needs never change. What they actually want a haircut to do never changes. The basic desires and wants and emotions that haircuts help with never change. A salon owner told me recently that it was different when I was a salon owner. The reality is it wasn't because people really never change.

Now one of the big things I discovered and one of the final things I discovered was this.

Whilst being a salon owner life was busy for me. I had one child after another until the fourth arrived. I had three salons at one stage, sold one and then another and I was also building myself a huge house in the countryside of Cheshire, England. Life was extremely busy for me.

Yet, the great discovery for me was this and I will tell it through a small story.

One day I was in a local village shop where I overheard a conversation. That conversation was about a man that had bought a large plot of land. That large plot of land was surrounded by fields, sheep and even had an apple orchard in the corner. Parked on the land was a mobile home where this man and his little family were to live whilst he built a huge house that was to rise from the ashes of a derelict building that housed a large pig and a horse or two. The people on this shop were talking about this man. One said he was a TV star. Another asked if he could be a music star and yet another wondered if this was a guy that had maybe won the lottery and was now investing into this land, house and far.

They all agreed one thing that the man must be rich and famous and all will be revealed as time goes on.

I knew who the man was but I didn't say a word. I paid for the things I had in my basket got into my car and drove around the corner to the large field with the large house where the man was living with his children.

I was that man.

I discovered that through hairdressing I could become exactly what I wanted to become. To most I was just a hairdresser yet to myself I was rich and successful beyond my dreams at the time.

I think one of the biggest things I have learned in the business is never give up. It's a cliché but it is also so easy to surrender to pressures once they start. So many times over the years I felt like saying 'screw you' yet the rewards of being a successful salon owner were so great I knew I could do it. There are times when you simply have to carry on regardless of how low you feel and never forget everything is different after a sleep. Tomorrow you'll feel very different, things will look very different and the situation that is on top of you right now will seem easier to solve I guarantee it.

You can do as you like, you can become what you want to become and your hairdressing salon can be as wildly successful as you want it to be.

Never forget nothing happens by accident.

I was the punk and I was the salon owner and I know exactly how it works.

So now listen close because I am going to show you how to SALON PUNK your salon.

There Are Basics Business Experts Will Fail To Tell You

I think the amount of experts around with no expertise is pretty shocking wouldn't you agree?

To give you an example it isn't uncommon for salons to come to me for help and advice that haven't already been to five or more 'experts' before. The salon owners have spent huge amounts for very little and in most cases NO return. Shocking –pretty shocking but with the advent of the web and the cheap access to creating a highly premium look and feel brand ... this is a reality these days.

It'll help if I explain why that is.

I met a salon owner who had a serious lack of clients coming through their door. They had been to an expert and had carefully followed the experts 'expert' advice. The advice was as follows and the advice is pretty common. I agree with none of them.

This is what is taught. This is what is wrong.

Create discounts to bring in clients especially through quieter times.

Dominate Google with SEO.

Set up a Facebook page and load it with content.

Create an Instagram page and take endless photos against a selfie wall.

Start a blog and write articles.

Load your salon with retail.

Change products, brand and change everything.

Build another new website.

Go for a refit to attract more clients.

Take even more cutting courses.

Order a high-end salon system.

And so on.

Yet, these are some of the worst things any salon owner could do I certainly would never do when it comes to making a fast impact and building your salon business.

So, when I arrived to meet the salon owner they had one major problem and that was a serious lack of people walking into their salon or calling their salon despite spending a small fortune and doing exactly what they had been told by the expert and previous experts.

The results were clear to see ... the salon just wasn't busy enough apart from other management issues we fixed!

And here is the strange paradox. Whilst the salon owner and the stylists were locked behind the open glass front into the salon, sitting and waiting for clients to walk in, checking their Facebook and social feeds many hundreds and thousands of people all needing haircuts every week would casually walk past the salon front door oblivious to what this great salon could offer.

All they needed to do was to get off their screens and convince the people walking past to come into their salon.

And the fact is none of what they had been told to do by 'experts' was working.

Here is why.

Everyone and anyone do the above in their salon. It can be done well but mainstream, most salons do it exactly the same – as the 'experts' have told them.

And despite the fact that this salon owner like many others was posting endlessly on social media from the protection of being behind a screen behind a desk the process of posting online was doing zero for the salon.

So if the clients are not pushing open your front door the solution is really simple.

STOP waiting for clients to come to you – you must go to them. In this case it meant opening the front door and making a connection with the people walking past.

Yet for some salon owners, they find this approach far too simple despite the fact I have helped to build half a million pound turnover salons from the ashes doing just this.

It seems a lot of salon owners these days are being bullied by the attachment to technology and being sold the easy sale of 'click and go' marketing. It isn't just salon owners of course it's the business world as a whole.

Yet the facts never change and it is this ... printed marketing will deliver far more than any online portal can deliver. Radio will deliver more. TV. will deliver more. Word of mouth will deliver more.

And the massive power of referral and sample marketing for me are still the king of the column building process when done right with a tight tested system to support it.

And the salon marketing systems that are built into our salon computers are also a problem. Why?

From what I have seen and read the majority of the messages built into the salon systems, word or strategic experts rarely put marketing tools together. Is there such a thing as an expert in writing marketing words?

In 2003 and once I left the word of hairdressing I fell into the world of strategic business building. This was a world I had been practicing with my own salons but had no idea of the terminology or practices of this world. All I knew was one word can make a difference to the reaction of the person reading the message.

For example a client came to me that was a salon owner. She needed new clients and needed them fast. She had been running an advert that was bringing in zero clients. I took her advert and changed the words and layout. The results; she emailed me in a panic saying over 400 new clients had responded to the new advert.

Recently, I also helped to put together a campaign for new salon staff. The previous advert had failed but overnight this new advert had the salon completely inundated with enquiries for stylist's positions. I simply changed the wording.

And finally another salon owner had very little response from the letters or emails being sent out from his salon system. I helped him re-word all of the letters. This change almost blew his phone off the hook.

Now tell me words make no difference?

The actual area of expertise is an expertise known as copywriting. An expert copywriter does this. If you ever hire a copywriter avoid going to cheap and ask for proof or previous works.

You should ask yourself, have all of my marketing materials my your salon system been put together by an expert copywriter? I doubt it from what I see daily. But the good news is they are easily changed.

So the fact that your salon system has a marketing suite doesn't really mean you have a marketing suite that is going to work. Just because I drive a car it doesn't mean I would win a formula one race.

And of course there is the routine or system of marketing. Most salons advertise a discount during slow times hoping to bring in a client or two. All this does is lower your average bills during a time when it can be hard to pull in the cash anyway. This can actually totally destroy salon takings for the week due to the fact that you have cut your income in half during a very slow time.

What Is Real Salon Business and Marketing?

A salon owner of over three decades told me he almost died of shock when I asked him to do something he hadn't done for over twenty years. His business was slipping and slipping fast due to overcomplicated marketing and poor management that just wasn't working. He like most salon owners are doing every new fad that clearly did nothing to build his salon business.

He did as I instructed him to do – reluctantly – and his salon business, turnover and clients started to rise! He was shocked, I wasn't!

Another salon owner had spent a small fortune on marketing agencies, marketing experts and just about everything you can think about to build their salon. After two years of trying many things their business was in decline.

After working with me for just four weeks business began to grow. After eight weeks many of the salon management issues were solved and after just twelve weeks the salon turnover was still increasing and had increased by an extra £3,000 plus every week.

And one more salon owner approached me. They had flyers, they had a Facebook page, they had Instagram and they had plenty of salon chaos. Within a four-week period not only did her salon stop the rapid decline, we had increased her salon turnover by almost 223%. Just an incredible result or as they said in a message …"INSANE"!

How?

I am about to tell you exactly what you need to do to fill your salon, keep it filled and make it grow at a rate you've never seen before. I will also tell you the essentials you need to add to make sure this happens and of course keep it happening.

This all comes with a warning and it is this. If it sounds too easy that's because getting a salon packed is easy. There is no science attached to this you simply need to give people what they are already looking for.

And despite the modern advances in marketing and tools remember this. Most of the salons and businesses I work with double, triple and even quadruple their salon businesses have been done in most cases without the use of the web.

After this chapter I will show you some real cases studies in action. This will help you to really understand how incredibly simple this will be for you to do.

And remember … break a rule or two it really is the only way.

Here we go.

So …

Understanding Why Are You In Business – Do You Know?

Out of the hundreds of salon business owners I know and have met most seem to know two things. First, they are in business to make money and two, they are in the hairdressing business.

That isn't true.

No one is in anything to make money. They are in it to bring into their life what money can buy.

For example when I was a hairdresser I wanted a big house. The only way I could get a big house would be to have a very successful salon. The more success I had the closer I came to buying a big house. Finally, I had the big house and the successful busy salon.

The other things we really want from our salon are happiness and freedom. We imagine that being a salon owner will and can make us happier and give us more freedom.

Yes this is possible but the reality is most lose their internal happiness due a lack of money and a lack of profit from their salon business. Once there isn't enough profit the bigger dreams like a house or whatever we dream about starts to slowly fade away. Once that dream has gone we are really in the week-to-week struggle of making our salon work or even dare I say – survive.

I worked with a salon owner that wanted more happiness. She had had the salon, almost lost her salon, her staff had all but gone and she wasn't taking enough money to pay for anything.

When I asked her she simply wanted to be happy again. The salon had not only destroyed her happiness but had also destroyed her 3rd marriage. She asked my honest advice.

Do I close it?

Do I start again?

Her debts were so high I was wondering if we could fix this yet I also knew it could be fixed as long as she worked hard in her salon to make it happen.

After installing previously proven salon systems needed to create a successful salon, after creating a new client program, management program and finding new staff, her salon not only restarted, built fast, and also avoided the past ten years of habitual mistakes that had almost lost her the business. Today she has a very successful salon.

Her goal? To get off the shop floor and build a real business. Today that is what she now has.

She was happy to open her salon all of those years ago. It very quickly made her miserable for years. Today she has found happiness once more by listening, taking good advice and building a solid business. Happiness is now hers once more.

So what you really want is happiness, freedom and of course a salon that can deliver great services, great haircuts and also can deliver you a life that you deserve for taking the risk of being in business.

Visualize Your Perfect Salon Outcome 12-Months From Now

Let's be realistic here. How many times on New Years Eve have you promised yourself your salon will be different this year?

You know what you say... "I can't have the same year as I had had last year", and then you make a resolution to really make it happen.

But what really happens after the first week of the resolution? Usually not a lot as you probably know.

The reason for this is a lack of clarity. You must be clear but also you must be realistic. I worked with a salon that when asked their perfect outcome over a year they said they would like to be able to turnover £5,000 per week. For some salons that isn't a lot and for others it is huge. They were taking just under £2,000 at this stage.

After looking at what they had in their business already I decided to agree that this number was very doable and in fact £6000 per week would be even better. After just two months not only had they hit their target but their takings are still growing and heading for £10,000.

How?

Partly this is due to two things.

The first is they have a set outcome in their minds on where they are now heading.

The second is they could see their potential with what they already had in place and could make changes to.

So a realistic aim or goal over 12-months is very doable as long as it is realistic for you.

For example if you only have two stylists, one and yourself and your cut and finish price is say £35 that gives you a possible potential of £100,000 if you are fully booked up for fifty weeks of the year.

But it would be more realistic for you to work out the numbers and then set your goal. Let me say this to encourage you. I have a salon that can easily turnover £4,500 with just two stylists right now. They have everything in place but had almost faced forced closure before we worked together. One thing the owner has is a fixation on his long-term goal. That goal is £7,500 per week and has almost hit it a few times.

So set your goal or outcome 12-months from now and at this stage base it on money or turnover.

The turnover should be built around

Paying yourself a decent a wage (not just being in business to pay for everything).

Every salon owner deserves the big reward. If you are not getting paid first and I mean before anything you will lose all motivation to stay in business and this in turn will destroy your happiness.

So the question is this; what is your ideal weekly wage that you would settle for from your salon?

You need to know your break-even (and more). This is the amount of cash that covers everything in your running salon effectively.

You absolutely must know your break-even number or the exact amount you need to take to pay for everything comfortably. This should include your wages, your bills, your rent, your tax – everything. If you are like me and not great with numbers there are plenty of Apps or software that you can use on your phone or iPad to work this out fast.

When working on a break-even I always add more on to the real number. This gives you a cushion and is a more honest approach to the numbers.

Stock cost Vs. Stock profits and margins.

Don't be fooled into thinking that last week because you sold £400 of retail that £400 is all of yours. Every retail company has it's own mark-up and profits. There can be bottles that you will make just 10% on and other bottles you can make 100% on. You must know that if you sell a bottle of shampoo how much of that is actual profit for you from the sale. I love retail in salons but there is more money in specialist services for less effort.

Taxes.

Most business ignores taxes or sees them as a burden. The reality is they have to be paid and can only not be paid if you are not taking or managing your money properly. Even a famous football player that earns millions upon millions each year decided he didn't want to pay his taxes so set up and elaborate scheme to avoid paying tax. This resulted in him not only getting a huge fine going into the tens of millions but a suspended prison sentence. I met a salon owner that turns over £4 million annually. Incredibly he is way behind on his taxes by hundreds of thousands.

I love paying taxes. It is my proof that business is going well and I have my numbers right.

I have been behind paying them when I was a salon owner to the point I almost lost my salon twice. I would call it the good old days but I would say they thought I was making a killing in those days and had all the good things to prove it, the big house and the German cars the lot. The reality was simpler – my taxes weren't getting paid and that is because I didn't take time to understand and know my numbers.

By the way it's worth sharing with you I am yet to meet a single salon owner that can tell me their numbers. The problem is when you don't know them your salon as a business is at risk.

So you must set your 12-month goal but this means you must know your numbers and this means doing what you might not want to do and that is sit and work out the number details.

If you don't know how to do them properly or where to start you must pay for advice to get help on this. It'll be the best £100 you spend.

Is your goal realistic and doable?

So now you have your 12-month goals in your mind. But are they realistic and reachable?

First - realistic.

If you set a goal of hitting £5000 per week do your numbers stack up and make it possible to hit that number? Do you have enough staff in your salon to make it possible? Do you currently have the skills to make it possible? Do you know exactly what needs to be done to make this possible?

For example when a salon owner comes to me and we go through their numbers here are the other numbers we need to know and understand.

What is the price of a haircut in your salon?

What is your salon average bill?

How much colour do you sell?

How many clients per week go through your salon?

How many clients per week do you as the salon owner service?

How many clients per week does each stylist service?

These are the numbers you have to know. If you don't know them you are working blind. If you are working blind you will not reach your 12-month goal.

A salon owner came to me and she told me her salon was doing really well. I mean she said she was doing very well. She has and had five stylists and herself servicing clients. The salon was and is very busy. She is at an age where she wants to get of the shop floor.

Because she cannot get off the shop floor she has less happiness and time.

Once I looked at her numbers that she kept saying were amazing I quickly discovered that her numbers on paper looked really good but they didn't make sense and I will tell you why.

As the salon owner she was responsible for taking the lead and setting the pace in her salon. Her column was packed and I mean not even space for the smallest light to shine through. Her column was also taking over 55% of her salon turnover, which meant she was killing herself on the shop floor to create jobs for underperforming hairdressers.

Yes, her staff is great and the money was coming in but this successful salon had redirected her happiness. Why? She hadn't got to grip with her numbers.

Another salon had a manager they loved. I mean they adored her personality, character and the way she would arrive on time in the salon and keep the salon clean.

The problem was this and it was bigger than they could have seen themselves. This manager was getting paid £500 per week. She was taking on average £625 per week after six months working in this salon. That wasn't enough to cover anything and the reality was this was just another case of a salon owner working really hard to create a job.

You cannot measure the success of your salon on staff with nice personalities. This is a business and you must know your numbers.

Any stylist absolutely must be taking through your salon at least three times their wage. So if a stylist is getting paid £350 per week their column turnover should be at least £1,050 or three times their wages.

I cannot say this one enough; if you fail to know your most basic numbers your salon could be on a route to failing. So take time out of your salon if you have to and get to grip with the numbers you need to know to build your business.

Assuming you now know your numbers make sense?

Let's get this as simple as possible.

Know what needs to go out or get paid?

You now have a figure?

Know what is coming in?

You now have a figure?

Now you have those numbers is it realistic to hit your new goal or will you have to make changes?

See the manager I mentioned earlier? After six months of taking just £625 I advised the salon to let her go. This is the kind of change you might have to make. I understand you might not want the hassle and battle to find new staff but believe me when I say once an old door is closed the new one will open. I have never seen that not come true.

Don't be scared of making the changes you might need to change to make sure your salon starts the road to becoming a business that will give you what you need in your life.

Once you know your numbers you should do this.

If you have six staff each member of staff should be treated like a separate business within your salon. This means you have six businesses in your one big business. Let me explain.

Now you know your numbers for your salon you need to know the numbers for each member of your team.

Recently I worked in a salon that had a team of stylists all sitting around not really doing a lot apart from the odd client here and there. The salon owner told me they were all busy. So I took the numbers for the salon but then the numbers for each stylist.

One stylist was doing really well but the others were all doing average.

The problem is if the stylists are not treated like small businesses within your business they are carried by other stylists that are producing well.

Your staff is all micro businesses within your big salon business and should be treated this way. This means that you need to know the numbers for everyone otherwise you will find that you might be carrying more than you think.

I went into a huge London salon. I mean it was massive. They had around 25 stylists but when I arrived the only person doing a client was the salon owner I have gone to meet plus a junior and a receptionist.

After he had finished I asked him where the staff were. So he took me to another part of the salon. Once we got there a door opened only to reveal a room packed with staff drinking coffee and swiping through their phones. He seemed ok that they were all in there. I was wondering about his sanity.

Never forget; you are not here to simply create jobs you are here to build a business that makes you happy.

Know your numbers – all of your numbers.

Knowing Your Staff?

I don't think most salon owners really know their staff. I was the same. Once I took on a young guy who was average but became great. His column was packed morning until night. I would have sworn he would be with me for life. I gave him keys, favors, loans, and helped him buy cars, houses and holidays. I looked after him.

One day I was off at home. I was in my garden and I heard a car coming onto my drive. It was this hairdresser. I could tell he had that 'I resign face' but tried to keep it friendly. He told me that he was sorry but wanted to hand in his notice. He didn't want to work any notice and wanted to leave right now. I asked him why? He told me his new boss insisted that he start on Monday. Monday was just two days away. This was after 7-years.

The point is you never really know your staff. Ultimately you are the person that pays them a wage but if it comes to the crunch staff will always put themselves first.

Now this book isn't about staff but you have to know and understand who your people are if you want to hit your goal. If you don't they will hold you back and resist everything.

I worked with a salon that had a team that had been there for a long time. Once we began to work together we quickly realised that his team were resisting every ounce of change in his salon. They never saw the point of main changes, they thought changes were bad for the salon and they didn't feel the need to do things any different.

So I dug a little deeper. It turned out there was a ringleader. The ringleader was a stylist that had become very set in her ways. She was also the salon manager. She had gotten to a stage where she didn't want to do anything in the salon and her takings had even gone from £1400 per week down to £850 per week. She had been there in the salon for over ten years.

The salon owner asked what to do about her? I replied give her three months to make the changes or she needs to be pushed out. Finally she left the salon and the effect to the salon after she had gone was spectacular.

The stylists were actually enjoying the changes but didn't want to do the changes because the manager made it clear she didn't like what was happening. She had gotten lazy. She also realised that if the other staff took action it would make her look even worse.

After she left not only did the graduates grow dramatically the salon turnover increased on average £3000 per week within weeks of her leaving.

You need to remember that staff can make or break your business. You need to remember you have a big goal that you want to reach. Staff are not there to be employed they are there to service the bigger idea of what your business will become.

Yes look after them, love them, be fair with them and give them what they need to do an incredible job but never allow them to control your salon at a level where your salon will start to suffer.

One salon I worked with, guess what we did? Fired everyone and started again. Why? If we didn't nothing would have worked. Today they have an incredible business and a really great hair salon.

Does your staff make sense when it comes to your bigger picture for your salon?

Is What You Are Already Doing Working?

I had a call from a salon owner. He told me this right up front. We are doing Facebook and Instagram, we do flyers, we have cinema advertising, we run newspaper ads and we do just about everything you can think of. I don't want to do any of that working with you.

I asked him do you have enough clients, turnover, new clients, and services and are you making enough profit.

He replied no.

What do you think?

Clearly he was doing everything but doing nothing right. In other words nothing he was doing was working. It can be so easy these days to take an easy route especially with marketing.

There are those experts that will tell you to load up your blog with free content or to keep posting on Facebook or social media but the reality is very different. I've seen a lot of marketing that has had a ton of cash spent on it yet it clearly doesn't work.

How do we know it works?

The numbers rise, stay the same or fall. It isn't rocket science.

I spoke to another salon owner that was told he had invest in SEO for his salon website and continually re-design his website. They did this for 2.5 years with no extra increase in salon business. In fact they told me not only was it costing them cash every month they also told me that their salon turnover had reduced significantly whilst working this way.

So you must look at what you are doing and stop doing what isn't working. This sounds and reads like common sense yet I think if I wrote every story of a salon that refuses to stop what isn't working you'd be shocked.

In a different industry I advised a company to stop doing what they were doing. The numbers and sales were down hugely. No new leads or sales of anything were coming in. When I went to consult and mentor them I saw in a moment what was costing them a small fortune and losing them a small fortune. I advised them to stop doing certain things right away. The cost every month went into the tens of thousands. After meetings that could take hours and then eight weeks to get a decision they concluded that it is better to carry on doing what they are doing for now because it was better than nothing despite the fact what they were doing was killing their business.

Why?

We all like to do what we know. We all like familiarity. We like what we can do. We even like it when it clearly isn't working.

The problem is when it isn't working is this.

Not only is it costing real invoices that have to get paid but it leaves a lot of potential business that is missed due to lost time, lost funds and lost directions.

So what now?

You need to look at what you are doing and ask the question 'is it working for me?'

For example; if you are using Facebook how many clients come to you through Facebook? If you are putting all of your marketing energy into Facebook and getting no bookings through Facebook why are you doing it?

It could mean a couple of things for you. It could mean that Facebook simply won't work for your salon business for reasons that you might not know right now. All you know is it isn't working for you.

Does that mean it won't work then? No of course not.

I have a client that used Facebook for years with no real results in business. I advised them to completely change the way they approached Facebook. Thankfully they did. The results have been astonishing with client bookings and questions endlessly being posted and followed by real bookings that bring in real money.

This is an industry that is ultra-cosmetic in its approach to everything – of course it is we are hairdressers. Generally marketing campaigns are based more on how they look rather than the message that is being projected.

Image is critical to us but image doesn't pay your bills. So it is critical we test, track and measure the results of our marketing campaigns. Doing this takes away the guesswork and allows us to refine adverts and campaigns to make them work and build our business.

I met a salon owner that had spent a small fortune on their salon. The fittings, the décor, the whole thing looked amazing! After 18-months they closed, what a waste and I wasn't surprised. They were average, did average and took advice from average. They paid the price of someone's bad – very bad advice.

If it isn't working why are you doing it?

What do you need to drop and stop doing fast?

What Needs To Be Done To Stabilize Your Salon?

Most salon owners tell me their salon is stable. Stability is usually based on money or turnover. The reality is very different. How about you?

As you've read staff or doing the wrong things can create very real or impending instability or a lack of cash and profit in your salon. But you might have to create some fast turn around magic right now.

A salon owner called me in tears and I mean after five minute she was hysterical. All her staff had once again walked out. She had a part-time stylist, herself and one junior. She had gone from a situation of thinking she was in control to losing control completely. This couldn't happen to you? That's what I used to think until it happen to me when I had my salons.

Not only did she have almost £20,000 debt and climbing her break-even number for the week was way above what she could take right now. After going through everything over a 2-day period a plan to stabilize her salon was put into place. The plan ultimately had to be cash that was over her breakeven figure. We managed to do this and over a four-week period her salon was now stable. That doesn't mean it was safe – it was just stable.

After a 90-day period her salon was not only stable but had a new team that was trained and taking really good money again.

How?

This is what I call direct action or a boots on the ground way of marketing. It simple, use or leverage what you have to create an influx of cash you wouldn't already have.

One thing I love to do with salons I work with is help to design and create campaigns and strategies to bring back masses missing clients. This works brilliantly well. Why?

Think about it the client knows you guys, she or he has been to your salon before and despite the reason for them not coming back that reason can be as simple as they forgot about your salon so it really isn't anything personal.

One salon started a campaign to bring back their missing clients. Over a three-week period they pulled back in over 65% of clients that were missing. Over a year we worked out that the missing clients were worth a potential £189,000. Another salon I work with increased their salon takings in a week by just over £1,400 by simply using what they already had and that is bringing back their missing clients.

Now if you are thinking that you cannot bring in those new clients how about this. This is based on the clients you have in your shop today, right now.

I have a stylist that has just hit £2,000 plus a week. It's taken around 16 weeks for him to hit this. When we started working with his salon his turnover was around £700.

How did we do that?

First, we planned it out very carefully with management and marketing changes. This also meant a new approach systemized consultation had to be carried out by the stylist. This also meant the stylist had to stop thinking too much like a hairdresser and more like a problem solver. This in turn meant the hairdresser could now offer more hair solutions rather than just simply doing a haircut. In a nutshell this meant, redesign – more cash – colour – more cash – Olaplex – more cash or the bottom-line is a hugely increased average bill.

His average bill went from a low £22 per week to as high at a peak of £171 after we worked out the system. This meant the salon turnover went through the roof without a single new client. We simply leveraged what we already had within our hands without spending a single penny on marketing or wasting a ton of time pretending to be incredible on social media. This is business – salon business at it's very best and most powerful.

Your most powerful ally if you need to make your salon as stable and stable fast is using what you already have.

He felt this was a risk.

I can tell you there is more risk in taking no risk! The results revealed that.

How Fast Can The Changes Be Done?

When I opened my first salon all the way back in 1989 I suffered from a serious lack of cash. I had just bought my first house for £14,500. I had also sold my car to fit out my salon. I was also expecting baby number one to arrive at any moment.

So when I opened my first salon, failure wasn't an option. I couldn't wait for results or cash to arrive. I had to be busy and had to be busy fast. This whole process taught me something very easily on and that is anything that needs to be done should be done as fast as possible. I never waited; I couldn't wait and just had to keep pushing everything through as fast as I could. I was never perfect – far from it – but it gave me results. Some did fail but a lot succeeded very well.

I always find it incredible when salon owners want to wait and see what happens. What does that mean and what does that say? Does it mean they are not bothered or can it mean they possibly don't trust my advice in a world that is pumped with so much distrust? Or could it be that this isn't the only source of income and the other source will pay for the bills.

Recently I did some very early work with a salon owner. I knew within minutes of meeting they would probably close. The shop had been open for five years. The salon owner had decided that although this was a slow salon the other salons could support it. I don't get that. I just don't get it. This salon was in a small town of just 15,400. It was also next to many other towns containing hundreds of thousands in population. Anyone with hair needs to have his or her haircut yet this salon was pretty dead.

They had four staff to pay and the running costs were pretty high. When I asked what they are doing they explained that they post on Facebook everyday. I asked what else they said they have a Pinterest account the post to now and then. I asked are they doing anything a little more direct. They replied no. They felt that contacting clients direct would hassle them and didn't want to appear to be pushy. This salon is now closed.

The truly ironic part is this salon didn't have to close. I have a salon I also work with in England. These guys are in a village surrounded by five miles in every direction of grass. They only have a population of 3000. Since working with me we saw the most transformative change I have ever seen in any salon including their best week ever in January when every other salon was sitting, hoping and praying for a client to walk in.

The point being this.

They refused to wait for something to happen.

They couldn't wait for something to happen.

They took every minute of every day to make sure that salon was absolutely packed from morning until night.

How?

They did what I told them because they knew if they didn't I would be kicking their Asses – and I did. These guys now have a 7-star truly EXTREME and truly punk salon.

So how fast can you turn your salon around? How fast can you take action? How fast can you start contacting your current clients or taking other actions to increase your salon turnover?

Here is something I discovered.

No one will do it for you. It is always a choice. You choose to get your salon packed or your lack of action is also a choice to let your salon sink.

Whatever choice you take you need to take action as fast as you possibly can. What are you waiting for?

Who Are You As A Salon And Do You Believe It?

Who do your clients think you are? Are you just another salon or are you the only choice of salon they would choose? Once you become an option or a choice you will struggle to stay on top.

When I opened my second salon I knew that there were around 35 salons in the town and many had been there over thirty years. I was new but I also knew I wanted to be the only option for hair otherwise how could I survive?

My mind was set and I set my thinking based on something called perception. I knew Mercedes or BMW were the best cars yet I had never owned, driven or even sat in one. I knew and felt the same with other things in life and this got me thinking. Why did I believe they were the best when in reality I had never had one or driven one?

This is called the perception of value or quality. This perception has to be based around what the client thinks about our business or service.

And here is the thing ... you have to TELL YOUR CLIENTS... because if you don't someone else will or even worse the client will guess and usually guess wrong.

So I created a huge ongoing campaign that I never stopped for a moment to create a different perception of my salon business.

I arrogantly told everyone we were the best. I told everyone we were number one. I told everyone we were unique. I told everyone we specialized. I told everyone why we did certain things a certain way. I also studied what all the other salons were doing and did exactly the opposite to what they were doing where and when I could.

And ... I never stopped for a minute telling them because I knew as soon as I did stop telling them they would forget.

This was a huge thing for my salons. I realised if I don't tell them they never know who I am or what I am about.

Recently, I worked with a very quirky salon that is doing really great things. They have so much going for them. Cool, quirky, fun and doing some really amazing hairdressing.

The problem is they weren't telling clients this so clients would walk in and see and feel just another salon. Quickly (in days) we made changes. The changes were simple things like information packs, information cards, messages on their social media.

Guess what happened? Clients began to talk to them about who they were and what they can do for them and their hair. This was a new conversation despite being open for years. This has also resulted in a large increase in their turnover weekly.

Why?

Perception is a powerful tool. You must educate your clients to know and understand who you are as a business. Are you just another one of many salons or are you unique? If you are unique how are you unique and are you telling people you are unique?

If you don't tell the client who your salon is believe me when I say the client simply won't know.

What Is Your Vision For Your Life? Life Is Short So Think About It?

Deep, but listen to this.

You are born and you die. The bit in between is the bit you must fill. How you fill it is a series of endless choices. Those choices are what will make a difference to how you live your life. This includes your salon life and salon business.

All salon owners open their salons with the best intentions but ... this is a huge but ... when it comes to making sure the salon delivers your dream business this can easily be given up due to daily pressures of running a salon.

This is when choices are surrendered to the grind or to the daily reactions that feel hard to control. They're not as hard to control as you imagine yet they need decisions that are in harmony with your life vision and dreams.

Now go back to the dream of having your own salon. I am sure you imagined that dream would be filled with all kinds of things that will give you happiness but has it? Has the pressure of simply running a salon almost crushed you at many levels?

When I had my salons I wanted the best of everything. I can't say I just deserved it for opening a salon but I wanted the rewards of a bigger business. I knew I wanted a huge house and that house eventually arrived. I knew I wanted a new BMW and that car arrived. I knew lots of things and los of things arrived. I thought about and I knew.

There's a reason this is critical to your success and it is this.

Having your vision and knowing where you want to end up. It's like a final destination or an arrival point.

Let's illustrate.

If you want to get to Edinburgh in Scotland you need to know how to get there. Once you know how to get there you leave in your car. Once in your car driving you will take a wrong turn now and then, go in the wrong direction and at times have to turn back and start again.

But you know that you want to get to Edinburgh in Scotland and until you arrive there you will keep going. This is the journey and the destination. It's you seeing yourself and your partner or family at that final arrival point. This is the vision you have for the journey.

Your salon is no different. You have to have a longer vision and see yourself at the arrival point. The arrival point is what you dream about.

What's included in your salon dream? That is up to you to paint the perfect picture. If you have no picture it's almost like jumping in your car and just hoping you'll arrive somewhere but you have no idea where.

Think about this.

What do you want for your life and can your salon give you want you need? This is where you have an opportunity to create a real business rather than just another hairdressing salon.

But like I have said before, it's a choice that you can take or not take. Either way it is a choice.

Let's Get Marketing Your Salon
– THE EXTREME METHOD –

All the marketing in the world will not give you a brilliant salon if you don't manage your business well. I recently met a salon owner with an incredibly low rate of just under 30% when it came to client retention. He thought new clients were the problem. It wasn't. The real problem was retention.

So marketing alone isn't enough. Yet if we are in a position where we feel our salon systems are tight marketing when done well can give you incredible results for your salon.

Now, I really want to stress this point and it is this. Most salons I work with, double and even quadruple their businesses have already been in touch with experts, they feel as through they have tried everything yet still have salons that are going from one disaster to another or are simply not busy enough.

So what you are going to read is so simple that you will find it hard to accept, as this is how you should do. At the same time some of the results I have had with my clients like: 233.7% increase in just 23-days. 53.4% increase in 28 days. 404 new clients from a single flyer campaign. £1,400 from one simple strategy. Salons saved from certain closure. Over 586 new clients from one strategy. New stylists going from £250 per week to £1,700 per week. Graduates going from being pushed onto the shop floor to being packed within 6-weeks!

Extreme and hard to believe numbers yet all true numbers from real everyday hair salons just like yours that were stuck, struggling or simply wanted to move forward and grow.

Let me make this as simple as possible in a world that makes everything as complicated as possible.

There are two things you need to know about marketing.

Direct response marketing

This is my own personal favored way of working. It is direct; the results (or lack of) are seen instantly. It is the most underused method of marketing due to its ugly or in-your-face nature. The returns are usually fast when done well.

Visibility marketing

This is marketing that is in it for the longer haul. This is a kind of marketing that is also wrongly used and usually used when salons are slow.

How do you know which to use? Easy, if you need urgent or faster results, clients and cash in your bank direct marketing is the route you should use. If you are in business for the long haul you should use visibility marketing.

Here's why.

I had a conversation with a salon owner. We spoke about increasing his business. He told me that he had tried Ads in the local newspaper with offers when his salon was slow. He also said it was a waste of money and did nothing to increase his business. He ran the Advert for two weeks then that was it.

I spoke to another salon owner. It was slow over the summer term. She decided to have 15,000 flyers printed and pay for them to be inserted into a local newspaper. There was a discount on the flyer. She said she wouldn't do it again. I asked her why? She told me out of 15,000 flyers not a single one had been brought back into her salon.

And yet another salon owner had been convinced to pay for Google Adwords and Facebook Ads. He replied that after 3-months not only had he not seen in increase in his salon turnover he had actually experienced a decrease.

There's a real process that takes place through marketing and advertising. The process is conversational. The process is awareness. The process is also a process of supply and demand. There is more that I'll break down and explain for you.

Let's go through what happens. For the sake of this example we will use a woman.

A client starts to think about her hair long before she contacts your salon. Her thinking is usually about changing her hair. That can be provoked by a life event like a divorce, a birthday and so forth. Or it could simply be she wants a new hairstyle and is maybe willing to go to a new salon for that change because her current stylist just does the same old thing.

During this process her mind makes a connection with a real need. That real need is when she looks in her mirror and keeps talking about her hair to herself.

"My hair needs to change"

"Should I change my hair?"

"When's the last time I changed my hair?"

"I love 'famous persons hair', would it suit me?"

"Should I have a colour?"

And so on.

In other words she is having a conversation with herself.

Now hold that thought that this client is talking to herself. Her conversation could have been taking place for months and even years.

So you would imagine it will be easy to get this person to come into your salon right? So if you post a flyer through her door or she sees your ad on Facebook this should be enough for her to come into your salon?

Well here is what you should know.

It really depends on whether you are stepping inside her current internal conversation and offering an answer to the questions she is already asking herself.

Now is this visibility or is this direct response marketing?

OK, let's break this down more and make it even simpler.

I recently worked with a salon that had as good as died. The staff had endlessly rebelled against the weakened owner. The owner was sick and tired of being sick and tired with salon life. She asked me honestly ... 'should I just close?' Her marketing was simple discounted Ads in the newspaper.

The need for income was really urgent; she had bills piled so high you could easily get lost in the panic.

What I did was put together a plan of action that was for the first four-weeks direct marketing. This meant we went directly to individuals or groups and made them irresistible offers. The offers themselves would have a time limit of just three-days so this way we could measure the response.

Her response after just four weeks was an increase of just under 60% in her takings and then up higher to just fewer than 120% in takings.

I did the same with another salon owner. They urgently needed more income. We did everything direct marketing over the first four-weeks. In just 23-days they had increased their turnover by an increased 233.7%.

Now please bear in mind both salons had already been doing 'marketing' but had no results.

Direct means we go direct. In other words if we have a customer base that we can use to leverage our salon turnover we do that. If we can create joint ventures and alliances with local business so that they endorse our salon, we do that. If we can hand out a flyer on the street with a take it now or lose it offer we do exactly that. This is direct, this is measureable and it forces the potential client to make a decision there and then.

If we simply run a newspaper ad because our salon is slow this rarely works. But if we run those ads to create what is visibility they can work.

So once your direct marketing is really working the next step is to make sure everyone knows your salon is there or increase your visibility.

Visibility is important but it isn't instant. You must be in this for the long term otherwise don't waste your cash. Why does this work so well?

It's a myth that advertising is for slower times and you don't have to advertise in the busy times. Not true!

Advertising during slow times keeps your salon in the eye's view of the public. Advertising during busy times ramps up your income dramatically.

Every year for years on the run up to Christmas I would advertise like crazy. I would talk about how great we were, the great things we are doing and the skills we had as a salon. I made sure that when anyone thought about hairdressing in our areas we were the only option.

Then when it got busy I also ramped up my marketing using direct mail, newspapers, flyers and just about any tool I could find to make sure all 125,000 population in the local town knew how to book their appointments. Year on year on year on year the salon just got busier and busier. Of course profits increased and I even managed to get off the shop floor.

Advertising is as important as making sure your scissors are sharp or your dryer is working. But – it has to be done right and according to a plan.

Have you ever seen APPLE doing no advertising even during the slow times? Any day of any week you can see Apple advertising their products.

The reason we need to do visibility is many but one being people quickly forget. We need to let them know we are there. We need to let them know why we are there and we need to let them know who and what we are as a salon. This means that in the most public of places your salon can be seen. This means that if there is a space somewhere for you to stick a notice or poster about your salon it should be used.

The more your salon is seen, the more your brand or salon is seen, the more your logo or tagline is seen, the more your work is seen and spoken about the more visibility you have as a salon.

Everyday in my own salon I had a list of at least twenty or so things that had to be done before anything else. I used to say to myself – 'Alan, do what makes money first'. Some brought money in right away but all were part of my daily visibility.

Recently I worked with a salon on visibility. Even after nine years in business they were surprised when they were told to ask on the street if people knew their salon. The surprise came when locals replied 'NO' they hadn't heard of the salon. We spent twelve weeks building and putting together a plan of action that including both direct marketing and visibility marketing. The results after just twelve weeks saw turnover climb and extra

£3,400 per week. I'll be excited to see what happens after twelve months.

Another salon I worked with decided to sign-up for six months of bus advertising. They wrapped the bus with a simple logo about their salon. Another salon invested in radio and saw results very quickly. Yet another salon I worked with invested heavily into local newspapers. After one year she finally hit her one million pound turnover. Before we did anything on her visibility her salon was very close to closing.

But of course whether it is direct marketing advertising or visibility nothing will ever replace the work you do on the shop floor. Do great work or train to do even better work and your clients will come to you begging for you to become their stylist.

And the reality is we are living in a time when breaking the rules, going against the grain is a good thing. In a world that is proud to push out the fake. Never has there been a better time for you to be truly authentic as a hair salon. Stop copying everyone else. Look for ways to gain distance between you and your competition. Study what everyone in your town is doing and do the opposite. This is the punk way, this is the strong way, and this is the better way for you to support your efforts.

Ultimately though you need to make sure the marketing you do has a return on your investment. Here is how I like to work. For every hundred pounds my mentor clients spend with me I like to aim for at least £1000 return. Your marketing and advertising should never be a cost. Never be like the salon that signed and spent a grand a month for one year only to watch their business decline through wasting cash resources. This is your salon, this is your business and this is your life. You have to be able to sleep at night and do the things all salon owners deserve to have. This will only happen when you are taking good money into your bank.

Real Case Studies From Real Salons – Fake News And Lies –Lol

This next bit should come with a warning but first.

I had an email from a potential salon owner that wanted to take part in Salon Mentor Extreme© but still had questions. Rather than ask me the questions he went to a very well known sales rep of a large cosmetic company.

He asked the rep about my numbers and results on my websites. The rep replied something like this...

"It all looks made up to me, I've never seen results like that in any salon over my 30-years..."

And with that the salon owner actual told me my results were 'fake' and called me a liar.

So this next part comes with a warning because the numbers you are about to read will read like fake news. Yet here is what I know.

And I will say this once more.

I have always been in business for my business to work. The way for me to measure if it is working is by my results. My results are measured in sales. No sales and no one eats. No sales and no sleep at night. No sales and my blood pressure will go through the roof.

This is all really simple – it works or it doesn't. Middle ground is the worst option. Everyone does middle ground and less. Most salons believe in average because averages are what they are being taught by average achievers.

So ...

What you are about to read is what I do all of the time with salon owners I work with. Some of what you read is extreme examples and I mean EXTREME! Let's be really honest going from £250 a week in a column to £1,700 a week in a column – in a short period of time - is a number any stylist or salon owner would die for. That is what you are about to read. The stories are all true, all verifiable and don't revolve around retails sales or discounts.

So take them as you read them.

I have decided to remove the salon names and staff names, as it was becoming time consuming a little complicated getting agreements from everyone so I have put down the results and what I did with them for you but the rest remains private.

Now before you read.

This is all do-able and possible for you and your salon. The only thing that will stop you doing any of this is you. No one else, nothing else, just you. Be responsible but even more; take small but huge steps to move forward.

And speed ... for salons and me, speed is always the key. Do as much as you can, get as much as you can and do everything as fast as you can. Speed is part of your key to prevent boredom or getting jaded or even losing your salon.

I couldn't wait weeks or months for results when I had four babies on the go that had to be supported and fed. I needed results there and now. How about you can you wait? Of course not and if you do imagine the business you lose over a month never mind a year.

So here they are, enjoy.

The young graduate from £250 a week to £1,700 a week

This is a killer story and a story of possibility that I have seen many salon owners resist. Let me say this ... a graduate is a stylist but still in training. Most graduates have a capability that needs to be encouraged, nurtured and released. This way they will perform for you. If you don't at some point release them onto the shop floor they will move on to a salon that will allow them to express themselves more fully. That leaves you going back to the interviews and being short staffed.

So, the salon owner had lost a couple of stylists and his manager. He told me about this young 20-year old that is still a graduate. After talking about her work he said she isn't good enough. He is an amazing hairdresser with decades of experience so he was measuring the girl against his own skillset. I encouraged him to forget the industry bullshit, rules and restrictions for now and give the kid a chance.

We planned it carefully knowing and understanding that we might have around four-weeks of hairdressing work that maybe wasn't quite as good as it should be. I do know this though – what we notice as experienced hairdressers from graduates the client rarely will notice unless of course it is an absolute disaster. Even then that can easily be avoided 99% of the time.

Anyway, we put a plan of action together and pushed her in at the deep-end with a client column. Despite the small amount of work that wasn't quite as it should have been she started to flourish very early on. I wanted to capture and encourage her youthful and internal enthusiasm and rapid growth process in an extreme way.

When we began this small journey her column would be taking around just £250 a week.

In under ten-weeks of doing as I had planned using my more Extreme Methods© and directed my salon owner she delivered a week's takings in her column of £1,700 in turnover.

Unreal. Unbelievable. Jaw-Dropping. Faking it? Absolute verifiable and true!

Worth remembering it's pretty rare to find stylists that are taking more than £1,000 per week through their column so for a salon baby this was just cool!

How?

We gave her a chance a perfect opportunity.

We made her believe everything was possible.

We showed her the door to her dreams.

We offered her real possibility.

And we encouraged her. We showed her love. We spent time with her and her work skills. We set the bar high. We set her targets high but to her these were just targets and we never mentioned they were high. We trained her to work on her averages for all services especially higher average services like colour and Olaplex.

This whole process was tracked and measured daily. The tracking encouraged the salon owner but it also gave the stylist a position to be responsible for hitting her targets. Tracing and measuring everything is an essential key to extreme change.

As I type she is still doing incredibly well with her now weekly packed and high-demand column.

From £550 a week to £2000 plus per week –INSANE!

This salon owner sent me his salon numbers. I noticed as the salon owner he was taking and performing very low.

We talked about it and I noticed he allowed the clients to make decisions. They would tell him as a hairdresser what to do. Another thing I noticed quickly was the fear he had of asking at the desk for invoices. So we re-invented and recreated his consultation process. This process took time to practice and get right.

He was to listen closely and then offer his honest, open and direct advice. He knew what would look amazing on the client but never felt as though he could really share that advice and changes without his client's permission or the client's request.

He discovered most clients want change – this means higher averages.

He discovered most clients wanted colour – this again means higher averages.

He discovered most clients want incredible feeling hair – more charge.

In fact he discovered so much that his column went from a fluctuating £500 to over £2,000 per week and is stable at around £2,000 per week.

How?

By listening very close to what the client was asking for.

By regaining his confidence and knowing the client was ready to change and spend in his salon.

By understanding that price isn't the issue regardless of how high it went it was a fear of a hair disaster that was the issue for the client.

By advising colour and creating new technique for client colour.

By advising restyle and charging for the restyle and colour or anything else like retail that went with the restyle.

By gaining confidence in his prices and his value.

Very quickly, in fact, in under a week his numbers began to rise very fast.

The first week we worked together his taking were around £250 as an average. By the time he had completed his Mentor Extreme© program his column was hitting £2,000 and above. He had also had an extreme average bill of £171. How would you feel asking for that at your desk?

This revealed a lot for me and it was this. Even the most experienced and senior hairdressers can make massive, fast and extreme changes in their columns when they want to.

Self-belief is a major key.

How to sell over 250 Olaplex services –OMG!

When I discovered Olaplex I couldn't believe more salons weren't selling it. £25 per shot has to be the easiest money ever. Most salons I deal with are selling literally a handful every week.

The one thing I noticed is that the price is a major factor for the staff. How do you ask for £25 for essentially what is a squirt of hair cream?

Well that is how hairdresser was seeing it.

So we did a little training on mindsets and mental buying patterns. This of course reveal something obvious that really isn't that obvious... the client is buying amazing condition, shine and hair health – not a squirt of cream.

So with a new approach to consulting we finally added this one thing and this one thing was powerful.

Ready? Here it is.

It was a question.

"Have you heard of Olaplex?"

The client would mostly say no and the stylist would explain the magical power of Olaplex.

One salon I worked with went from selling two Olaplex a week to selling – 27 in a single week. Shall I tell you what that is in cash?

An extra £675 at the desk and all they had to do was ask a question. The client would reply yes or no.

Easy right?

Here's what we learned.

We have to think like the client thinks.

We have to tell client what client need.

We should never assume what the client wants to pay.

We should never assume the price is high for them.

We should never assume they'd never pay the extra.

We should be trained and try different approaches to make sure what we are doing is working.

And

Get as much FREE support as possible from our suppliers. The more we sell the more discounts we demand so we increase our profits.

Now imagine this.

Going from just 2 to 27 Olaplex services in a single week and with takings at £675 from the new weekly Olaplex sales.

If that kind of extreme momentum was maintained for a year that means an extra £35,100 in turnover from a little squirt or two of cream! That's a vision worth thinking about don't you think?

What's stopping you?

New clients up by a totally mental 583%

This salon had 2% new clients. That isn't enough to grow and would eventually mean certain closure in the future. So how did we increase those new clients from one a week to over forty in a single week?

The big myth is you have to endlessly advertise for new clients – you don't. But you do have to do something. Some salons hate advertising of any kind and want to simply attract clients. Believe me some salons do just that and they do it incredibly well. My wife always went to an indie salon in London. Prices were high, staff looked like rock stars, you couldn't make an appointment so at times you'd have to wait two hours for a haircut. The chance of getting a request stylist was slim unless you sat and waited forever. They were and are packed.

But they are the unusual. Most salons I work with struggle to get new clients and feel the only way to get them is to discount or advertise. This as they say is fake news.

Let me say a line about discounting. It will destroy your salon long term and is very difficult to reverse. There is a blog all about this on www.salonpunk.com worth a read if you haven't read it.

So how did we pull in over forty new clients in a week and growing?

Easy!

We simply asked every existing client to bring a friend or family member that hadn't been before if they would bring a new client into our salon. This took confidence, patience, training, and trial and error. Some staff didn't like doing it and some loved doing it. The potential was huge and over 64 new clients in a week was a result for sure.

But look at this.

The average bill in this salon was £41.50. That meant an extra £2,656 based on the averages in a single week in that salon but it was higher – much higher because they are also selling Olaplex, restyles and other client demand services. In a single week this salon had increased its turnover by over £3,000.

Like I warned you – unbelievable – extreme and mind-blowing numbers. No wonder a long-term rep advised a salon owner what I do was made up numbers. Yes to most they are but the reality is this is very do-able for you and your salon by making simple changes.

Would you like that?

You know time and time again I see this stuff as so simple. It is a little effort and some extra training. If you can do that you can increase your salon turnover very fast.

Extreme Salon turnaround in 12-days that was NUTS!

This was a salon that was going to close at the end of the month. Now image this.

She hadn't been paid for months. Debt was spiraling out of control. Her staff wages and stock were a struggle to pay. She couldn't pay her mortgage. Can you image the pressure and stress and sleepless nights? I get that because I have been there and it freezes you to the spot so that it feels like nothing is possible.

It's worth sharing what she was doing to get busy. It wont take me long to tell you because it was one single thing.

Social media.

She has spent what look liked forever investing, spending and posting on social media with no results to show for it yet she carried on posting hoping that what the 'self proclaimed experts' were telling her was right. It wasn't it was total business bullshit that was destroying her salon.

Let me get this out of the way. Stop allowing amateurs to advice and tell you what works in your business. I have been working with real businesses including my own since 1985 and I can share with you I have seen many an expert still get paid as he or she watches the business they advice to slowly crumble under the amateur advice. I have also seen business fold under bad advice. You've been warned.

So here is what we did.

One word.

EVERYTHING we could.

We stopped ALL online activities right away. The reason is being over connected actually disconnects you from your client base. She had become totally disconnected with what customers wanted.

Here is what I believe. If you are drowning you do everything you can to stay alive. You grab everything and refuse no help. It is an extreme moment and a moment that has to be grabbed by both hands and feet where possible. No exaggeration this is survival.

So for me ... we use everything to reduce the risk of trying things that might or might not happen or work.

Here is how the world of most marketing and ad agencies works. They pull out a top-drawer plan they use for everyone. Like a blueprint. They then start the long drawn out process of putting your plan together by pretending it is bespoke for you when in reality it's the same as what everyone gets apart from the new logo they insist on. The even bigger problem is it can take a minimum of 3-months to get anything moving.

This salon was hanging on the edge of a cliff by its fingertips, it was trying desperately you keep its head above water... months was out of the question, this had to be in days and weeks.

Here's one thing a lot of salon or marketing experts understand online. Being online is about two things. First is traffic or visitors and the other is conversion. For every salon online in most cases you need around 100 visitors at least. To drive 100 visitors to a website or Facebook page has never been more difficult. Some pages are getting literally a handful of visitors weekly. This will mean a dramatically reduced amount of clients if this is where a salon focuses due to the low conversion ratio.

Likes isn't cash at the desk.

Shares aren't cash at the desk.

Views aren't cash at the desk.

And posting content unless it's seen, read, targeted and studied will do nothing apart from devour your time and efforts and of course money. This will kill your salon.

To start with for this salon we spoke to people, sent letters to people, created simple visibility flyers, stood outside her salon, stood outside her local coffee shops, created small ventures with other business and had as many daily conversations with as many people as possible.

A sample program was created and supported with a referral program. The sample program never meant free as the upselling for other services had been trained practiced and relentlessly pursued. After one week of doing this the salon takings had gone from £950 to £2,300. Let me stay this once more.

IN A SINGLE WEEK from £950 to £2,300 in real money taken at the desk and put into the bank and all with NO social media or online efforts.

EXTREME to say the least! She called me in tears of happiness. I had tears for her. What a truly exciting moment. This salon was now not only about to survive but also about to stabilize, thrive and grow and it did even as I write this salon is killing it with takings of over £10,000 every week at our last conversation.

How?

We had to stop everything that was being done in the salon to supposedly build the business.

We had to rethink the whole process.

We had to STOP the endless addiction to posting on social media the same as what every other salon was positing.

We had to get creative and create a new approach locally.

We had to let the whole population know we are there and know we are the best at what we are doing.

We had to change our own habits, which isn't easy but was done for the sake of survival.

We had to change the way staff were working and reacting to clients.

We had to make sure everyone understood the purpose of sampling and a referral program.

We had to have a strong vision and self-belief that everything was going to be fine but we had to work really fast to make sure this salon survived.

And of course after the salon was back on track they continued their social media using a new approach that increased their fan base and customers dramatically.

The change was dramatic. The change was extreme. The effort not only saved her business but also saved jobs and serviced the city with amazing hairdressing.

How to get inundated with cvs from the best hairdressers – THIS IS FAIL-PROOF!

Staff is a real problem and every salon I work with has that problem. Yet for me the problem is incredibly obvious. Just look at the terrible job ads. Yes they look amazing but the fact is unless you know what a stylist is thinking they will never apply for the job.

One salon I worked with asked if I could help them get staff? Yes was my answer.

Let me explain.

A young stylist was told she would get £300 per week plus training and bonuses. She was even told she could get discounted products and other salon related benefits.

I asked the salon to actually ask her what she wanted. Her reply was this.

I want my own apartment.

The salon was fixated on – the salon.

The stylist is fixated on – their life.

There are two different mindsets going on.

The salon owner was surprised and I asked why after all what do you want from your life?

So once we researched what staff really want (by asking them) we changed the whole advert to reflect this.

Whilst all the salon ads were saying the same old thing my salons have strong adverts that are 100% focused on the staff. Why? Because if you give people what they want not only will they arrive but the chance of them leaving are very low. Yes some will live but it drops dramatically.

So if a stylist can get things like (just ideas) …

Manage to get their first house or apartment.

Their first car or motorbike.

More time for themselves and family.

More days off or Saturdays off.

Flexible working hours.

More clothes, technology or the things that they want or feel they need in life.

Possibility of more money and all the usual things people really need in their life.

We ran ads that reflected this and in one week a salon had nine new and high quality applicants into their salon. That is a result for a salon that had just one poor applicant the previous two months. This is a fail-proof approach that I have used time and again with my Salon Extreme© salons.

Just saying the same as everyone else isn't going to work. Getting extra training, working with this brand or that brand isn't enough you have to consider the lifestyle of hairdressers and what it is that humans want from life. Once you know you can deliver this proposal in your advert but be flexible with any offer you put forward in your job ad.

How?

What you need to remember is you are not employing stylists you are employing human beings with real needs that have to be filled. Unless you give the applicants what they want from their life hairdressers wont apply. In your ads you have to become the only option rather than just another any old option. When you are any old option they will stay until the next best thing comes along.

Keeping your stylists for years and years and even longer

I used to lose stylists all the time. One year or 18-months after I had spent time and money investing in them they went. Nothing has really changed but I want to share with you the answer to the age-old salon question ... how do I keep my stylist?

Here's how I solved it and here's how I kept all my staff for over a decade. And here is the same thing I advise all of my salon mentor clients to do.

This is a short one but it's the truth...

Give them what they want.

That's it.

Find out what they want and give them what they want.

For example I employed a brilliant hairdresser who had just had a child. She had everything I wanted in my salon but she asked for something I didn't want to do. At this point I was still hiring and losing staff so she was just another stylist interview at the time.

This was also the stage where I really started to understand what I wanted from my salon and team yet I felt I still needed staff that would be there all the time. You know, 9 AM start and finish at the usual time. She had a request and it was: I am interested in the job but I want to start at 10 AM and finish at 4 PM 3-days a week. I also need to have at least one Saturday off every month to spend time with my family. Sat the time I felt confronted by her reasonable demands but then realised if I give her what she feels she needs she will be perfect. So the job was designed to suit her needs but at the same time it had to suit my salons needs also.

This was the first time I had made major changes to a job description. It was also the first time I really changed the way I worked with my hairdressers. My head was in the place where I felt that I had to have every hour god sent from them so I had to make a switch to if they deliver what I want from them then everything is fine.

She was the best hairdresser and manager I ever employed.

She got everything she wanted from her job.

I got everything I needed from a brilliant hairdresser and manager.

She over delivered time and time again during her work for me.

She stayed at my salon for years and still stayed when I sold the salon to the new owners.

I then simply copied what I did with her to all new hairdressers from that point. But there is a key and it is this. You must know what you want in your salon before you give anyone what they want. What they want has to be in total harmony with what you want from your salon business.

One of my top guys I even helped buy a car for him and his first house. He stayed with me for over 7-years.

This is how and the only way I got my hairdressers to stay with me. They loved it and I tried my best to love and look after them when they worked for me.

Learn to be flexible with people and loosen up more.

Accept new challenges from staff and work with it rather than against it.

Allow more from the modern millennial and make sure you understand their needs because their needs are very different to the previous generation.

Don't resist big wages as long as there is big money to be had if your stylist is delivering. I stick to one simple rule and that is a stylist gets paid around 30-35% of what they turnover. If they turnover £2,000 each week will you really have a problem paying them?

Start with a strong plan in your head about new staff and what you are expecting from them. Don't just hire and hope it all works out – that becomes a hire and fire scenario.

Remember it isn't all about you. Yes you give them a job but in return this is a value exchange. They give you what you need as long as you give them what they also need.

This worked for me for years.

It'll work for you just as well.

Stick with the up and downs and you get this right and I guarantee you'll never lose staff again.

Screw social media and start a real salon marketing campaign that works

Despite what you are being told social media isn't the Holy Grail for your salon. You've already seen what I said earlier. You know how I feel about this. It isn't that I don't like it – I do – but you have to look at this very differently. This is good advice based on what I have tested over the years here.

Once I did some work for an art gallery. They had a famous painter visiting so they had promised to send over 300-500 people through the gallery. The more people – the more paintings get sold. Just ten days before the opening they had booked only around a dozen visitors. We created a campaign for this and did some interesting tests. I am happy to share with you, as it is a same result as I have seen with salon social media ads.

The gallery wanted pictures of his paintings used in the ads. I didn't want to use this. I ran this ad with another ad. Same words but a different picture. I tested their picture of the paining against a picture of the artist paining in his studio. He looked cool, tattooed and had his triumph bike in the gallery.

The picture of the paining had just 4 click-through. The picture of him painting had almost 300 click-through. This shows that if you get creative with your photos and posting you can get the desired effect. He had his 500 visitors into the gallery and all partly due to the photo testing.

So as you can see I am not against social media I am simply against using JUST social media as a way to build you salon. Marketing research reveals that print marketing still out pulls social media. In some areas social media results are so low they are no longer registered as a result and have seen companies move away from social media as a way to build business.

Get smart and stop dreaming that scrolling and thumbing your phone is going to build your salon, believe me, it won't. The only way I have had extreme results with my salon is to do everything possible to make sure your clients see everything. For me I am still not seeing these amazing promises on social media. I am still not seeing the numbers. I am still not seeing the promises coming through.

If you want a busy salon you absolutely must get out there and meet people. If I was building my own salon right now I can assure you of this – I would NOT use social media.

Ask yourself this.

How different is my social feed compared to other salons?

How many bookings to I get through social media everyday?

How much cash per hour I spend on social media does social media bring into my salon?

How much of my valuable time does social media steal from my real efforts to build my salon?

Can I list at least 10 more effective and extreme ways to build my salon business as against social media?

Get Off The Shop Floor By Breaking Your Arm?

The most common thing I get approached with is the above...'Alan, I want to get off the shop floor'.

The good news is it can be done. Is it easy? No, but it can be done.

A salon owner approached me. His main goal was to get off the shop floor. He felt that simply hiring more staff was the key to getting off the shop floor. It wasn't. The key is systemizing your salon.

So we started the process of systemizing.

He had a manager already. The manager was the usual manager that had been promoted simply because she had been there longer than anyone else. Her income into the salon was average but high. Her management skills went as far as opening and closing the shop. Let's be honest you could train a 3-year old to do that but the 3-year old would never be a manager in a million years.

The first thing we had to do was to create an outcome in mind for the salon owner's life. No point starting anything unless you know where you are going. Then we simply started to put into place or construct systems that would make sure the salon owner would get off the shop floor. The manager had to be replaced with a manger that understood the dynamics of management. Then the owner simply had to manage the manger rather than the whole salon.

Eventually after time the manager text me from a foreign land. He told me he was taking a month off with his partner to do new things and enjoy his life. One month later he returned to find his salon doing as well as ever.

When I had my own salons getting off the shop floor was a dream. I was the salon owner that was doing over half of the weekly income despite all of my staff. I was also the salon owner that was working more hours than any member of my team would ever work. I wanted time to do my own thing and be around to bring up my young kids.

After many managers, many fails, many issues and minor disasters I finally managed to get off the shop floor but there is a story behind this I'll share for the first time.

My column was insanely busy. I had clients that I had been through births, marriages and deaths with. I had clients that I did their hair for their first wedding and their fourth wedding. Their obvious commitment to me was painfully hard to break. I was part of the family and part of their life. Breaking away from the shop floor was never going to be easy.

I decided to break my arm.

Not literally but I decided that if I wore s shoulder sling into the salon and told my clients that I had broken my arm this would give my clients three-months to get used to another stylist.

I walked into my salon and told no one what was going on. I simply told my manager to move all of my clients as I had broken my arm. She was in on the plan but no one else knew a thing.

I would stand at the desk and explain when I could. All of my clients were sympathetic and happily went over to other staff for now.

This was extreme (and dishonest ... forgive me) but my reality was I now had more time than I could ever handle. As soon as I got into my office upstairs I would throw off the sling and sit and build my business.

Here's the thing.

Once I got off the shop floor not only did I have more time but I spent the next few years doubling and more my salon turnover.

The more I did on the shop floor the less time and money the business generated.

The less I did on the shop floor (zero) the more time and money I had to live my life.

How?

You have to learn to let go of the need for being wanted by clients.

You have to accept the clients will be fine with another hairdresser.

You have to understand that this is business and business always needs changes.

You have to know what you want and why you want it.

You have to create new systems based on what is working rather than try to reinvent.

You have to become the strongest leader you have ever become and separate yourself from your staff.

You must have self-belief that this is doable and can be done fast.

You must be willing to rebuild a team that is in total harmony with what you now want from your salon.

You have to wake up and accept that your hairdressing salon has to become and act like a real business rather than a hairdressing salon.

You must understand that a business is a serious business and should be treated accordingly.

Your salon become a business when you treat it less like a salon and more like a business

Everything is possible in your salon. Some of the examples I mentioned are extreme. I have met and spoke and seen enough salons to see a serious lack of results but a serious want for more results and changes. Everything you want from your salon is within reach for you but you must make changes in the way you think and then the actions you take.

This is the difference between a hairdressing salon and a salon that is an incredible business.

Building your salon isn't just about motivation, courses or being the best hairdressers. It is about defining your salon vision and journey and working on it accordingly.

I went through the struggles of learning everything the hard way and at times was lucky to survive. You don't have to do that but you do have to do something. Having a Facebook account or a flyer won't build your business but have great systems and strategies will.

All of the above are real. All the numbers are accurate. All are verifiable and true.

Any one of those numbers can very easily be you and your salon.

Ready To Change - SALON PUNK - Your Salon The EXTREME Way?

Ready for change?

Are you?

Have you had enough of mediocre, average and same old hassles?

Yes?

OK, lets do this.

To SALON PUNK your salon you will first need to change the way you think at many levels.

I've said this once and I will say it once more; if everyone is doing it, it probably isn't the right thing to do. I have never built a salon business doing what everyone else is doing. Most businesses follow the fad or what is in. The problem with that is that it isn't tested to see if it actually works. Can you risk doing that? I know I couldn't.

Marketing for salons is now sold as a science. It really isn't. It's simple and it can be done by anyone. However there is a big reason most salon marketing no longer works for so many salons and it is this.

The past years and more saw the arrival of the web. Before the web to find and get expertise we had to either search for it or discover it through trial and error. I came from a period where I had to try everything and hope it would work in my salons. Some of what I tried failed; a lot of what I tried worked incredibly well. To hire a true expert in those days was expensive for me. It was expensive for anyone.

Today it is very different. We live in the age of personal significance. Everyone wants acclaim and adoration from one source or another. This has created a huge wave of self-proclaiming salon experts with no real expertise. This can be a huge and destructive problem for salons. I know because I've seen it first hand.

You can now create the most incredible websites for free using many tools online. Creating an eBook on salon business as a subject has never been easier by plagiarizing or hiring a ghostwriter.

So suddenly we are in a world where you have to choose between endless streams of people claiming to be experts in our industry yet have no expertise of the industry.

Why is this an important thing to say?

But most salon owners that come to me have already tried many 'salon business experts' before they get to me. That expertise has failed them and cost them hugely. They have also tried just about everything you can think of to get their salon message out there and still failed to see the increases in salon business they want.

This reveals two huge problems taking place in our industry.

Misinformation from misinformed experts that are simply selling what they have read about elsewhere. This is an over complication of what marketing really is in our industry.

Let me share with you some of what I see on the front line of our industry and I will start with a story. This story might sound a little repeated from earlier but it is without a doubt a number one issue I am seeing with salons today.

A salon owner rang me and eventually booked a site visit. Once I got to the salon she welcomed me and invited me into the salon to see what was going on.

The salon was absolutely totally dead. Her staff was in the back room drinking coffee, swiping through their small screens and maybe waiting for a client or two to walk into the salon. She stood behind the desk and then explained to me about the huge amount of time she was spending on Facebook and other social media to build her salon.

She complained that learning the Ads system was complicated but she was managing it. She told me she loved her Ads in Facebook and they looked really nice. The same with her Instagram obsession, her twitter start-up and her relentless battle to give away tons of free blog content and finally what she called Google domination.

She told me she loved doing this, loved her Facebook presence and loved the look and feel of her social media.

So I asked her a question.

'Does it bring paying clients into the salon?'

She smiled and said 'yes.'

I asked her 'where are they?'

She replied, 'maybe it doesn't?'

She really didn't know.

There wasn't enough cash to pay wages, invoices, stock and even staff. Even worse she was earning not a penny from her salon when we met.

Now here's the thing.

Her salon is on a main street. It is also close to a huge marketplace. It is also next door to a famous coffee shop. It is also next to a car park that can host over 1000 cars. As I stood speaking to her an endless stream of people walked past her large shop front. Not one or two but a steady stream of people.

I asked her this.

'See those people outside?'

She replied, 'yes.'

I told her, 'switch off your computer and let's persuade them to walk through your salon door'. She was nervous and didn't want to do this.

Over a 7-day period using what the salon owner already had we created a week in her salon that I doubt she'll ever forget. That was done by simply switching off the salon social media and speaking to people face to face.

The problem and danger with social media and the web for your salon is this. More connection and more engagement has created a real disconnect and more disengagement than ever before.

It has created reliability on a detachment from people that actually have a real need to be attached, engaged during the very personal process of touch, feel, smell, conversational art of hairdressing.

So one of the very first things you should do to SALON PUNK your salon is ask yourself are you making your marketing complicated because you are told it should be complicated?

Another issue that can and does hold back salons with marketing your salon is the issue of fads.

Fads have their place but like all fads they come and go and then fade to become part of the bigger marketing picture. Some fads might not be right for your salon. For example I went to one salon and the salon owner had around many many many social media outlets connected to his account. Anything new that was released he downloaded and used it. He was now at a stage where the management of his Apps was taking away time from the real issue of bums on seats and clients flowing throw his salon.

And just because it is there it really doesn't mean it has to be used. For example I spoke to yet another salon owner that started to get endless complaints about his use of SMS to market his salon almost every day. The software company had built it into the system so he felt compelled to use it. Yet the reality to push his salon SMS just wasn't working for him yet – he still used it.

And before we move forward who is it that is giving you instructions on how to build your business? Have they built salon businesses before and are they doing incredible things with their clients?

Here is what I know from hairdressing since 1982 and owing and running three of my own salons. The simpler and more direct, honest you are with your client approach the better.

If you want to SALON PUNK your salon listen close, take plenty of notes because what you are about to read are the steps I take my salon mentor guys through. Nothing is fixed or set in stone but this will give you a good idea of how to ramp up, fix, repair or SALON PUNK your own salon or turn your hairdressing salon into a real business with real results so as to give you a real life or life you really want.

Now of course I can't share everything here that I have done with all of the salons I have worked with, that just aren't possible and I will tell you why.

When I work with salons the salon owners like you they can call me every minute of everyday, or everyday of every week if that is what they need. A lot of issues are the same yet the fixes can be unique to their salon situation.

I always take an EXTREME RESULTS SOLUTION and a very direct route to fixing any salon problems and that includes clients, turnover, salon management, staffing, systems or more. This is also very unique to every salon so it isn't possible to share everything here as I think you'll understand.

For example, I have literally saved salons from closing. This is very different to helping salons grow.

Recently one salon I worked with we simply agreed to work on a figure that would stabilize their income and turnover. After just 23-days their takings had gone from £1,700 to just over £5,000 in one of the slowest months of the year – January!

With another salon we set a longer time to hit the figure and have worked hard to get everything in place. The big problem was management. Now that is fixed we can move along and work on numbers.

Another salon despite being busy had no new clients coming across the door. This meant they could not grow and add new staff to their team. We set a vision and worked on a target to start the journey. I helped them increase their new clients from none to just under 100 new clients in under 4-weeks.

So you have to know what it is you want and need for your salon right now. This is the most effective way to build your salon business fast.

This can raise another question; what are a want and a need? Well the answer is easier than you think.

Write down a list of what you want. This want might be a list of over 100 things for your salon. Now go through that list once more and ask yourself this question. Do I really need this or just want it?

A want is a desire that we can live without although we want it. A need is very specific to us and we really do feel as though we need it.

One salon owner will tell me she wants a million pound salon yet what she really needs is her salon to survive, grow and then once stable think about taking it to the million pound level.

Another salon owner I worked with really wanted a full-scale salon retail shop at the front of his shop. He had the space. The sales rep had offered nice shelving, top labels, support, training and a discount to get into his salon. And the truth is it would have looked amazing. But at this point this was just a want not a need. The salon needed clients, it needed numbers and it needed more cash in the till. This was actually his real need at that point. If he had gone for the retail deals do you think he would have been able to pay the large invoice once it arrived?

Another thing to consider with your salon is something I always consider when working with a salon and it is this. This is the easier way. This is the faster way. This is the key to EXTREME results.

It will always be easier to work with what you have right now rather than what you don't have. You have to maximize what you have rather than try and create something from things you just don't have. So we will look at what you have right now and show you how to maximize this.

Finally, there are a few keys things you need to know to truly SALON PUNK your salon.

These are the three very powerful salon keys I work on. Each key has many smaller keys within but this is as basic and as simple as it gets on paper.

1. STABILIZE –your salon
2. GROW – your salon
3. INNOVATE – your salon

Stabilize Your Salon

You must make sure your salon is stable before anything is done and I mean anything. That means it has to have the ability to feel safe feel good about owing your salon business and be taking enough cash to make sure everything is covered.

This helps you sleep at night. This makes your life happy. If the salon isn't stable you cannot grow or innovate your salon. If you try and grow or innovate your salon this will result in the salon failing. Being stable is one of the most important keys for your salon.

How do you know of your salon is stable?

One of the easiest ways to measure is always the numbers. Are you taking and banking enough money at the desk? Are you getting paid for all the stress of being a salon owner? Are your bills getting paid? Is your salon rewarding you? Are you struggling with staff? Are you lacking in clients? This and more will have a yes or no answer. Stability also is something that just 'feels' good and right. How does your salon feel?

Grow Your Salon

Once your salon is out of any danger, has released any pressure and won't tip or fall over - stable - you can then make plans to grow. Growing takes strength and energy. If the salon isn't stable trying to grow the salon could make the salon tip over into the abyss. So we must ensure your business is stable before growth but once stable we then aim to grow in steps you can reach. Growing a business can inspire you into bigger better and stronger and of course when done right it can also multiply your happiness.

How do you know that your salon is ready to grow?

Easy – is it now stable and do you have what it will take to grow? You need money or investment to grow but it will also take time and energy. Are you ready to grow your salon? Plan well and carefully. Get good advice to reduce waste of cash and losing time and even worse – missing out in sales.

Innovate Your Salon

To innovate successfully you need smart brains for ideas and of course funds to make this happen. Innovation takes time and establishing the new innovations or services through your hairdressing business. This again takes energy and funds and the most important is that of brilliant ideas. If you are not stable or experiencing growth innovation can be fatal. Tread careful when innovating and always get good experienced real expert advice.

Each key has its place and each area should be secure before moving into next.

Again

1. Stabilize your salon
2. Grow your salon
3. Innovate your salon

Before taking you deeper into on how to SALON PUNK your salon you should consider this short story of a salon I know.

They have a large busy salon. The salon owner like all of us wants more. And why not we work hard for our businesses.

His salon is on the edge of town but he felt that it would be better to be in the heart of the town. So he eventually signed the lease for another premises right in the heart of the town. His reasoning was that someone would buy his current lease and he would be able to very easily move just half a mile along the same street and have a bigger salon with more space and be right in the heart of the small town.

Over two years later that new premises has had a sign on the front saying, 'coming soon'. The rent is very high, the rates are high and other outstanding bills are high for his empty shop. It is still empty, still unfitted and still untouched since he signed for it. This could be the end of his 2-year old salon unless a miracle now happens.

Why did this happen?

See the three keys above? Each has a right time to make them happen. He felt he knew better and this has put his business under a tremendous strain. What should have been a momentous period in this salons life has become a dangerous tipping point that could end his business.

Whatever you do ask the questions before you do anything.

Now, there are forces greater than what we know. This even applies to the salon business. This applies to the invisible feeling you or your clients have. This in turn influences how people feel about your salon or even you. You should make every attempt to be as natural, as kind, as good a person and as brilliant a hairdresser than you can ever imagine.

This in turn will help attract clients into not just your salon but into your life and environment. This one thing can change a lot of things for you. Start all of your days with a smile and eagerness to serve others.

This is your opportunity to shine so brightly people will be talking about you and your skills and your incredible business for years to come.

Work pays off; hard work pays off even more. Yet the power you have in your hands as a hairdresser is enough to transform the life of another human. Just imagine that for a moment.

Know your own value, discover your own value if you don't know it and then and only then will your clients truly value you and your salon. The value exchange is a process driven by feelings. The value exchange is absolutely priceless.

The same can go for your salon business.

Listen closely to what you are going to read. Take notes and apply everything you read your salon. And of course ... break a rule or two in the process. Always do your own thing and stick to the salon punk ethic... questioning everything for the sake of your own growth and self-improvement.

Question everything

I went to a salon that was a total utter and almost complete disaster. Nothing was working and I mean nothing. The salon owner had now lost every member of staff apart from just two. I will say the salon owner had a serious attitude problem and didn't really treat her staff like I am sure she would want to be treated.

This owner just couldn't understand why after being in business over 11-years everything was such a struggle yet the reality is – there must be a reason?

To find that reason, I stopped everything, actually closed the salon for one week, and questioned everything that was being done now and had been done before we put anything else into place.

Finding the problem we easier than you might imagine. Fixing the problem was then done. The salon was now ready to become stable and ready to move forward once more.

Stop Everything

There are times in life when you must stop. A forward motion on your salon business isn't necessarily a motion towards success. It can be like a train that has no driver. The train still moves forward yet it's out of control.

I have seen so many salons like this over the years. The salon owner wakes up in the morning, drives to their salon, opens the door and gets frustrated that the salon is slow. They do nothing about it apart from sit and wait and hope for changes. Guess what happens? NOTHING – nothing at all!

One thing I like to do with my salon owners is this.

Find out what goes into their minds each day. The volume of images, words and messages through an iPhone or smart phone is now huge and never been busier. Everything you look at your mind must subconsciously process. The reality is your brain isn't as super human as you might think. The feed and flow of information can be so huge that it actually dulls your senses and stops you thinking with real clearly.

In a generation where we are encouraged to engage and connect this has created more disengagement and disconnection from a daily reality. The real addiction of being online has become a serious problem for those that want clarity of thought.

Now the thought of switching off your phone might sounds unrealistic for you yet if you want clarity to fix your salon you must regain the control and power of your mind. The mind or brain is a muscle. That muscle can be neglected or abused. Swiping through endless junk online is abusing the power of your mind. Allowing your mind to recover and rebuild is what creates your strong mind.

Here are some things that over indulging things that will distort your mind and the distortion will affect your salon.

1. TV
2. Facebook and social swiping
3. Emails
4. Too many opinions
5. Online 'experts'
6. Netflix
7. Alcohol
8. 9 episodes of Game of Thrones one after another ;-)

9. Carrying your phone with you everywhere (even to the toilet, shower or bed)

So if you want to solve your salon problems you must first do the following;

You must create a clear mind.

A clear mind gives your brain more power.

A strong brain will help you have more clarity.

More clarity will give you faster salon solutions.

The salon solutions will come thick and fast.

And of course like all good punks you should, question everything at this stage with questions like:

Why are we quiet?

What is the real problem?

What is causing this problem?

Is the problem less obvious than I am thinking?

Can the problem be fixed?

Why is this not working?

Why is this working?

Why am I not growing?

What do I need to do?

What new things do I have to learn?

Can I ask for help?

And other questions that are relevant to you.

And remember... the solution for your salon is in the silence. So if you truly want to solve any problems in your salon you must give your mind moments of silence to find the solutions.

Then and only then do you make a start on making the real changes?

Stop and really question everything.

Vision For Your Salon

Before you do anything you need to know where you are going. Only a fool would jump in a car and drive. Once stopped and asked where he was going he would reply ... I am driving somewhere that I want to get to.

The other person would ask where are you heading?

The driver would say as long as I am driving I would get somewhere.

When I first meet salon owners there is one question I always ask and it is this: what do you want for your salon? The reply is always the same ... to be busier. But what does that mean? Is it a reactionary reply or is it a reply that shows you are really thinking about your salon business?

Your vision is the result you can see in your mind. Like the racing driver that wants to win he sees himself holding the cup or the climber that wants to scale Everest he or she can only see themselves at the top. That is the vision. The vision is your final outcome of what you want for your salon.

In my experience working with hundreds of salons a salon with no vision is going nowhere. I knew for a fact once I had my big salon that I wanted to hit the No.1 position in a town of 35-salons. I also knew nothing would stop me. Yet I had to realise that it was going to take a lot of work to get there.

My vision was a little like this.

- N0.1 salon in a town of 35 salons
- Be the very best at what we are doing in our salon
- Have as much fun as possible in the process

Basic I know but I knew if I did those things the rest would follow.

In other words you need to have a rough idea of where you are heading – your vision. If you have no idea where you are heading you are actually going nowhere. Even better is this – know EXACTLY where you are going.

So to create your vision you need to give it a little thought. Some salon owners I worked with once we went through the process of creating a vision come back with answer like...

- More time with my children
- More time to be with family
- A bigger salon with more staff
- To increase the salon turnover

Yet to hit any of those targets as part of your vision you need to make other things happen. Over the past few years the rise of vision boards has become rampant.

So has the rise of the law of attraction and other ways to get what you want without doing too much work. Now there is nothing wrong with those things but I can tell you this from very personal experience unless you actually do something NOTHING happens.

I have never seen a tree grow unless a seed is planted.

My advice at this stage to you is this.

Think about your vision for your salon.

Make as real as it can be in your mind's eye.

See it as real and accept nothing less.

Make the time period for your vision over a 12-months' time period

Break those 12-months down to small time slots that can all be tracked and measured.

- Do it by the week
- Then by the month
- Then by the quarter
- Then by the year on year

Your vision is very personal but make it as real and as reachable as you can. A huge salon and tons of staff doesn't everyone on. Some of you just want enough money to enjoy a nice life. Either way creating an initial vision is the first step to making your salon more successful.

To generate an incredible salon you must have a vision for your salon in place.

Do you?

Review Everything In Your Salon – For Gods Sake Just Do It!

This is the stage that you now must look at everything and honestly ask yourself what is and isn't working.

The first thing I do when I meet a salon owner is look at and find out as much history as possible. That history can be 6-months or it can be 30-years. In both and all cases they have come to me because something is no longer working.

The biggest issues I see today with salon are a failure to manage and marketing the salon properly. Facebook isn't marketing and neither is Instagram. Not to say they don't have a place they do but it takes a whole lot more to get your salon busy.

But the point is if it isn't working the real question to ask is why am I doing it? It's so easy to fall into the trap of this is how things should be done yet the reality is if it isn't working why are we doing those things that aren't bring results for our salons?

I look at a salon and try and be as honest as possible. Ego has to leave the room and honesty and bluntness has to take over. That honesty has to be based on what we know is working elsewhere or in other salons. Even if we don't know what is working in other salons we can still look to successful businesses to see what they are doing and how we can apply what they do in our salon business.

One salon I worked just couldn't get their numbers up. The salon owner was focused on client numbers only. He was advertising like crazy, pulling more people into the salon and still couldn't understand.

The review revealed the problem was actually the staff. They were massively underperforming and the salon owner had also lost control of his staff. The rot had set so I advised one course of action.

The staff were given time to change. If they failed within a short period they would be replaced. We replaced all of them and built the most incredible team. Not easy but that's what we did. The salon owner now had a successful salon.

Your review should cover everything.

The Plan Of Action Is What You Do Now To Get More

If you don't plan everything is far too random.

You might take cash, you might not take cash, you could get busy you might not get anything anytime soon.

I spent years walking into my salons hoping certain things. Then when certain things never happened I was wondering what the hell was going on. The truth is a lack of a plan wasn't really destroying my salon business it was just preventing my salon business from happening.

It's easier to plan than you think.

When I go into a salon and start salon mentor extreme I have to ask questions before any kind of plan can be put into place. Once I have my answers I can then get started on planning and directing my results.

I start most of my plans with an outcome in mind.

For example I went to one salon and our outcome for 12 weeks was to hit £5,000 in turnover (from £1,900) and then a plan to hit £10,000 over 12-months. This is the bog plan but not it has to be broken down into smaller plans. With the plan problem have to be solved and issues in your salon have to be resolved.

Here's a rough list of what I have on one of my lists for a salon.

- Is the problem with staff and attitudes?
- Is the problem with managers that do not manage (common issues)?
- Is the problem with a lack of leadership in your salon?
- Is the problem the quality if services just aren't good enough?
- Stop what isn't working and start again if needed
- Fix what needs fixing as fast as possible
- How do we stabilize the cash to get the salon steady
- Find one thing that creates more for the salon
- Ignore the web until the business is stable
- Social media eats time and brains does it need reduced
- More retail products won't increase your sales – review this
- Mass coverage marketing needed for visibility
- How can we increase the client average spend
- How can we increase salon clients
- Do they have a sample program

- Do they ask for referrals
- Is there focus on salon and stylist averages

The above is a tiny list I gave you as an example. Of course your salon is unique and will have it's own unique problems. That needs solved.

I have one salon that was doing really well they just wanted to increased their takings in the group by £400,000.

Another salon also doing well had the goal of getting off the shop floor. Another new salon that was struggling wanted to survive.

As you can see every problem that needs a solution is unique to you.

So create a list and work through that list by asking honest questions of yourself and your salon business.

The Marketing Shift That Affects Your Salon – CRITICAL INFO HERE

Salon marketing has fundamentally changed forever. Most salon owners don't realise. Most experts have no idea. Never has there been a more important time to step back into the more human side of salon marketing. Like when the doctor sits and asks and listens, like when my mum would sit and ask and listen and like how I would sit and you guessed it – ask and listen. The changes are monumental beyond what I can say here.

The same old salon strategies and tactics that has been advised, shared and used for most salons are no longer work for most. The only rule in salon marketing is that there are no rules anymore. There is no top-drawer one salon marketing system for all. The shift is momentous but not really all that unusual when you understand why.

My mum did marketing without any thought. It was pure intuitive. Serve the need and fill the need. I tried to take it a step further in my salons, serve the need, fill the need and innovate within that need and it worked like crazy.

But everything has changed. I started to notice changes maybe five years ago in my own business and of course within my clients businesses. They had been taking place long before then but it had become more than obvious then.

What was always working was now no longer working. The old systems for salons, the tricks, the techniques and the absolute fundamentals of marketing were no longer working where they used to always work.

Then we have the social media marketing rampage, fads and time-wasters where everyone and anyone advises that social media is the best and only way to build a salon business. It isn't and from the results I have seen (some do incredible with social media but they are the few).

I have two clients I can think of right now that heavily invested into two big social media platforms. After 18 months one client made a change and went more grass roots with his systems after we met. We maintained his social media but took a more direct approach using old school direct mail, magazine Ads, forum Ads and some other tricks. Before we met his appointments stood at just one a day whereas after they rocketed to 17 a day.

That raises the question of why he persisted for so long over social media and his only outlet to build his salon business? The reasons is always simple and it is usually because clients like him are taking advice from so called 'salon business experts' yet the experts haven't done enough research into the journey within the mind of the buyer.

And feedback from salon owners like you supported that conclusion and awareness that massive changes in marketing and results had imperceptibly been sweeping through the world of salon marketing without the world of salon business taking notice.

Recently when asked a majority of those questioned replied that they didn't trust marketing people. Salon marketing and business experts had now adopted the role of the car salesman or they would do anything, say anything, and promise anything and anything but deliver in their results. The results have become impossible for those that are simply selling car – selling – and have no real idea of what takes place during the process of what a client thinks before they book.

Buying anything including haircuts is a real intuitive process that includes so many invisible actions before any buyer arrives at your salon. The initial idea they have, the thought, the search, the mind process and many other things that take place before the buyer decides to buy from you. I spoke about that with my mothers approach and my own approach within my salon businesses.

And recent years in the industry of salon marketing have been destroyed by the abuse of power handed to marketers where they have had the ability to blind people like you with what can appear like magic. The magic in fact is usually a simple process that hasn't yet reached the eyes and minds of the mainstream. The marketer has simply read what to do in the instructions and is doing it. The main problem is the promise they present when doing such magical arts.

Yet.

The problems for salon marketers and business go far deeper.

Here's why.

Marketing assumes that buyers want to buy and yes they do want to buy but not always from persuasion. Persuasion has always been 'A' force behind selling. TV is a great example of that as are some older forms of advertising. Persuasion is a set standard of buying from the mind of the seller yet here is a reality check – you cannot force anyone into buying anything unless they want to buy. This includes a haircut. Persuasion will not force the cash from anyone and when it does – and sometimes it does – a refund request is asked.

I remember years ago my own brother coming back from Spain to announce he had done something stupid. He had signed up for what was then called a time-share apartment at £400 per month. This was clearly higher than his wages yet the experience of going through the time-share process persuaded him into buying. Thankfully the legal process was such that a refund of his deposit was eventually returned. And if the buyer does refund you can bet they'll never be back again. I wonder how many people smile and say it seemed like a good idea at the time. The reality is it was never a good idea it was simply manipulation through persuasion.

Even hair habits have gone through a huge overhaul. Now with the power of a smart phone we have selective and addictive thumbing over and past your salon marketing materials. I used to tell my clients they had 3-seconds to grab a client via their computer screen. Today I doubt if you have one second.

The addiction is huge. You've seen people everywhere walking around, sitting down, on public transport and even with a lover with their faces fixed firmly on the screen before them. It's like a scene from a zombie movie. Some marketers see this as marketing nirvana after all if they stare at the screen you can gently slip an advert passed them and they will click on it.

No and here is why.

Addicts are conscious of nothing whilst being conscious of what serves them in the way they see service in that moment. Addicts also have selective choice playing its part like all viewers have that choice. It is anything but a marketers dream. The addicts can be so tuned in or so zoned out he selling opportunities is very few.

And those that are just thumbers, they scroll left or right or up or down or anyway the screen will go. In that moment the only action they care about is that they are taking an action with little reason with their thumbs. Today in my coffee shop a guy stands in front of me. He takes out his phone, opens the screen hovers his thumb above a small panel and does nothing but put his phone back into his pocket. Eventually he touches a panel. Facebook, email or whatever, he thumbs very quickly through everything without seeing anything and eventually stops. He repeats the same process until his coffee is ready. Once he picks up his coffee before he walks to the chair to sit he opens his phone so he is thumbing as he walks.

In the coffee shop itself I would guess around 70% in here right now are staring at a screen. All addicts or thumbers! Either way do you think persuasive salon marketing to minds that have their minds on something or nothing is a workable idea?

You'll say no yet marketing men are still pushing the idea that these are perfect people to sell to via social media. They're not.

Another things with Thumbers is this – they are extremely protective of their digital space. They don't want to be invaded with ads in what they feel is private and their own place. Their place is their screen in front of their eyes. This is his or her place where no one else is allowed. It can feel private almost secret. The last thing they want is what marketing men can advise which is to hit them in their pocket directly into their smart phones.

We have to remember people aren't stupid and can see right through it when they are being treated as stupid. The salon business is no different.

The old way of salon marketing could get away with treating people as stupid and to be sold to yet those were the days of the uninformed. Now people are smart as their phones suggest and have been made smarted by the huge volume of instant education online.

If you want to get more clients booked in there is a new way to do it and it is nothing like the old way. Marketing as you might know it is dead. I believe there are things coming that will make anyone in the marketing service industry almost extinct yet the marketing industry will have you thinking others for – as long as they can.

The Mental Millennial Mind Shift That Affects Your Salon Right Now

Staff isn't quite what they used to be. There's a reason. It's called millennial.

When I was a stylist I wanted the usual stuff in the day. House, car, garden, holidays and decent wage.

Millennial don't think like that. They stay at home or flat share. They get a bus or metro and don't buy cars. They no longer have holidays they want extended experiences. And the money? It usually comes a long way down in a millennial's list of priorities.

And also staff is heading into the job later than ever. As I write my own daughter has just started her year three in hairdressing and she is twenty!

This is also a problem than can be fixed but you need to be like a tree in a storm and have the ability to bend rule that are so fixed you will probably fight them to the bitter end.

Sophie comes for her interview. She wants the job but she has arranged to go away in October for 2-months travelling through Vietnam. She wants to start her job now and come back to her job when she gets home. She also wants hours that allow her to get the slightly later train into work, which means she wants to start work at 9:45am.

During her interview you have the feeling she'll be great so you offer her what you can as far as money goes but you are not willing to give her 2-months to travel and her late start at 9:45am. As far as you are concerned she has to take her first client at 9am and she has to be here like everyone else to build her column. You think money will turn her on but the reality is you missed it during the interview when she said money doesn't turn her on.

You want her to start; she wants a job that fills her needs. Money isn't a big deal as she lives at home and isn't interested in moving out anytime soon. All she really needs is her gadgets and her freedom to do, as she likes.

She doesn't want a job and has never thought about a career. She just wants enough money to create her life the way she feels like she wants to create it. If you cant and won't support that she will go elsewhere until she gets what she needs. She's a hairdresser but that isn't top priority.

This is the millennial and they are nothing like how humans were made last century.

This is a huge problem if you don't get it and refuse to get it.

It's a massive advantage if you do get it and support it.

Because if you give these guys exactly what they want from their job and as long as they are giving you exactly what you need from them as a hairdresser they will be the best staff you ever employ.

This affects your salon business and could affect it even more over the next few years if you fail to tune in to what staff really want.

And here's a warning for you: fail to get this and you are going to have a serious problem employing young hairdressers.

And Salon Management Urgh!

This is a real short one.

Get a grip and stop expecting your salon to run itself.

I swear it took me years to get this idea or concept about managing my own salons.

I trusted in staff. I trusted in reps. I trusted in companies. I trusted I training and I trusted in a lot of things.

Until I realised this one simple thing…

… I HAD TO manage my salon.

MANAGE IT … MANAGE MY SALON because nothing and no one was going to do it for me.

In other words YOU MUST run your salon like a fine tuned machine based on what is tried and tested to work if you want results that you want.

Opening a salon isn't managing a salon. Just like building a car is driving a car. It has to be driven and your salon has to be managed.

I've said this once or twice and I will say it again YOU MUST manage your salon like a real business. That means from the staff to the numbers to all the other things that make your salon a success.

Here is the one thing that transformed the volume of clients that came into my salon. It was a list written on a sheet of paper. The list had around 20-plus things that had to be done before 10am every morning in the salon. The list had to be signed when completed and filed. I would check the files each day to make sure these critical things had been done.

Be warned a lack of management will give you a very average salon or at the worst a salon that has to close.

If you just don't know how to manage your salon buy books, speak to experts, copy success from other business. Just make sure it is tested and proven to work.

Manage it please.

Your Salon – Your Business – Your Life Is A Choice

I started my own hair journey in 1982 when I went to college. Of course as teenage punk it began before then. When I closed my last salon in 2003 I was still learning about getting my salon busy and busier and still learning what it takes to build a business using good salon management.

I think the truth is you can never learn enough of anything when it comes to building your salon business but I did learn one thing so big that it changed the way I think about life never mind business forever.

It was this.

No one will do it the way you want it done.

Let me say that again.

NO ONE WILL DO IT THE WAY YOU WANT IT TO DONE.

You can hire whom you want to take over your responsibilities. You can hire staff; hire marketing people, hire experts, hire gurus or just about any other fix you think will fix your salon.

But if you are not in control ... you will lose control of everything.

The biggest issue I see in salons time and time again is the staffing side of things. It isn't the over expectation of what staff should be doing after all if we provide a job and a wage in return for that job, we as the salon owners deserve value in return.

But the big issue is really this.

It is a lack of understanding the needs of staff in your salon and a lack of training of what you want from staff in the salons.

In simple talk.

What your stylists or staff want: You need to know what they want their job to give them what they want.

What you want from your staff: They need to know what you want from your staff as a stylist or team member in your salon so they can give you what you want.

When position isn't clear and isn't done the salon can and does very easily breakdown. I have worked with so many salons that are hiring, firing and still trying to get their big break even after years. Yet if the situation with staff isn't fully fixed you can do all the marketing, have the greatest in salon computer, be great on social media and believe me you still wont see the results you really need to turn your salon into a real business.

And that business of turning your salon into a real business is also a people business. You staff are people, your clients are people and you of course are a person. So it is how you deal with very real humans on a very human level is what will determine how your salon business builds.

The second thing is systems. Systems are critical and another big and common issue for salon failure – or success. A system can be as simple as who makes sure there is coffee always in the salon? Who makes sure there is enough change in the desk for payments? Who makes sure every client is offered a drink? Who makes sure everything that should be done is actually being done in your salon?

Think about this. To be the number one salon isn't as simple as saying we are the number one salon. Being number one is an idea that has to be supported by actions. The actions are the plan. The plan is the things that have to be done to make sure you hit your goal of being number one. Let's say you want to double your salon turnover? Is just saying it enough? Of course not there has to again be a plan.

The plan can be a new idea you want to try but if you try it and it fails this can and will set you back. The plan can also be a tested route that has worked for others and with small adjustments will work for you.

Do you take the new idea that is untested?

Do you take an old idea that is proven?

I never liked teachers. I hated school. I dislike authority and don't like being told what to do. Yet once I discovered the power of learning what I really needed to know to get a result faster it changed my hairdressing business (and life) forever.

In the early days of my salons I read about an Indian restaurant that had decided to send letters in the mail to their customers. Before they could do that they had to collect the names and addresses of those customers. Once they had collected enough they began to mail the customers. The result for the restaurant was very significant if I remember it well enough.

So I took this idea (the tested plan) and decided to do the same two things. Remember this was before the computer age in salons. So I decided to start collecting names and addresses in my salon. After one week I had maybe 100 names and addresses. After two weeks and more they started to build nicely.

I then re-read the Indian restaurant story and experience. They had a special three step series of letters. So I decided to write a series of three letters. The letters were packed with spelling mistakes but I sent them to my clients all the same.

The letters focused on appointment reminders and were sent at five weeks, six weeks and then seven weeks. Doing this one strategy in my salon literally blew my phone off the hook in the early days.

But here is the point. It wasn't anything new; it was old marketing practice that had been used in a completely different industry. But it had now become part of my town salon domination plan.

That takes me to another issue I see in salons and it is this. The endless quest or push for the latest thing in marketing your salon business. The 'experts' are great at selling us this stuff but the real issue is do you need it and for me – has it been tested and proven?

Why take a journey with an unexpected outcome? Again, do you really want to use an untested plan?

And finally your mind; don't think your mind doesn't have the power to do things you think might be impossible. It has that power and more. But think about your mind. You will keep your car clean but do you keep your mind clean and uncluttered?

We are living in an unprecedented time where the mind can be filled with endless images, conversation and chatter from no one and nothing. We are getting information about lives and businesses that really mean nothing to us but we allow that information to pass into our minds. This creates clutter and can remove clarity from our thinking.

If you want a salon that is successful you must spend time clearing your mind, being of a single thought. That thought should be focused on your aim for your salon. That aim has to be sure that your salon is a success at the level you want it to succeed.

Here's a tip that has worked for me for years. Spend the last few minutes every night writing notes into a real paper pad on what you can see for your salon. I would sit and write, be number one, have the biggest place, have the best stylists and of course the cash turnover.

Doing that every night fixed it firmly in my head. I still do the same today with everything I am planning or working on. That was years ago but today I still do the same and I still get my results.

One problem I got hooked on at one stage was going to bed with my phone. I eventually realised that it was confusing and mixing up my thinking. I would even dream about things I had seen online. Today, I never sleep with my phone in the bedroom and have all sound or vibrations switched to off so as not to be bombarded with unwanted thoughts.

The other day my son stayed over. In the morning I took him a drink of tea to wake him up. I noticed his phone was on his pillow next to his head. He said he always goes to bed like that. I asked my other kids the same. They told me they all go to bed with their phones. I ask most people I meet and they at times can reply in total horror at the prospect of being asked to leave their phones outside their bedrooms.

Yet the reality is this if you want to have the ability to do more with your salon you need to take action. To take action you need time and freedom of thought. To have time and freedom for thought you need to literally steal back time from the things that want to steal your time – like phones and social media.

Just know this.

If you want to turn your hairdressing salon into a real business you have to take fast action and make it happen. Stop thinking it through, just do it. No one will do it for you have to do it. If you don't know how to do it you should get advice, you must get directions and you should listen to that advice if it is tested and proven.

And of course you have the inner you. The person and voice that tells you if you are right or wrong or can do things. This voice is so silent that you can know what you should be doing because that voice is telling you but you are just not doing it.

That is a choice.

Yet the greater choice for you is to take your salon to places you'd never thought even possible in the past.

I know this.

I took a new salon of my own from 250 sq. ft. to 2000 sq. ft. in just 18-months. It was never easy and a lot of the time very hard work. But the rewards were amazing. My salon gave me what I really wanted from my life at that time. It changed my life. It changed my family's life and out of 35 salons in the town we took the number one slot.

That took hard hard work. That took effort and it took work and effort every single day. This is a cliché but if I can do that I believe anyone can do it.

You can do it but you must get your plan, take action and actually make things happen.

Finally life is life. Life is a period of time where we can create the most interesting, unusual or even spectacular. It has drama, tragedy, surprises and triumph. We see new life arrive, grow and develop. Sadly we even see death and all of the sadness surrounding death.

Yet life is also your blank book. It is a book that you can fill with whatever you want to fill it out with.

Your salon story is part of that book. If you had to write out the chapters now how would it read? Is it the story you really want to read? That is your choice of course but just know every choice can become another choice if that is what you need.

I wish you well and I will ask you to let me know exactly what you thought about what you've read here.

Peace, love and be prosperous and kind.

Alan Forrest Smith

About Alan Forrest Smith
& SalonPunk.com

Hairdressing is in my blood. I can't escape regardless of how many times I might have tried.

I love it.

I hate it.

I love it.

Today I live in between Manchester, U.K. and Tbilisi in the Republic of Georgia (next to Turkey and Russia) with my wife Tamuna.

Since selling my salons I have always been involved with hairdressing salons at many levels. Apart from the hairdressing industry I have worked with literally hundreds of new businesses, old businesses, corporate businesses, startups, struggling and business that just demand more. Most of this work is done through my other site at www.orangebeetle.com where I built a strong reputation as being an experts-expert in more results and response.

Also I write fulltime as a published author of many books on philosophy, business and breakthrough topics such as finding happiness.

Salon Punk© is a child I adore. I love helping salon owners create happier places to work and service their community.

Hair is the most wonderful of things. It can create a smile or enrage tears. I will never underestimate that power.

So to finish here is a few things you might not know about me.

I lost my big adult front teeth at the age of ten when I fell over whilst wearing a large brown paper potato sack from head to toe and landing on my face.

I saved a man's life on a beach in Spain. He had drowned and I pulled him out, gave him the kiss of life and he came back to life!

I proposed to my wife early one morning in bed and said to her... 'Shall we go buy a ring then book a flight to New York? She asked why and I replied... 'Marry me'. She said 'yes' (thank god!)

I once saw a vision of a giant whilst with a Shaman in the Amazon forest in Ecuador (TRUE).

I once lost everything I ever owned in my life through a catastrophic divorce as recent as 2010. I was broke, homeless and looked like death! By mid-2010 I had designed a new life that looked exactly like I wanted it to look.

I used to worry about what others thought but eventually realised they were all thinking the same thing. I discovered that the only person I should worry about was myself. If I were fine those around me would be fine.

I love motorbikes.

I love tattoos.

I love my wife.

I love life.

That's it ... for now anyway.

Alan Forrest Smith

Here's my other websites.

www.alanforrestsmith.com

www.orangebeetle.com

More From SalonPunk.com

Salon Extreme21©
BEST SELLING SALON BUSINESS MANUAL.

You might just want more ideas on what to do and how to build your salon business. our BEST-SELLING manual Salon Extreme21© (21-days to grow your salon business) does just that. It's almost 500 pages in size, it's a large A4 folder and it is designed to be handled, read, written on and copied for the tons of salon management, salon marketing, salon business building idea. What else can I say apart from salon owners absolutely love it, we ship it all over the globe every week and the feedback is pretty amazing. Order now. The MAX delivery time is 15-days depending on where you are. UK delivery is around one week.

SALON BUSINESS CONSULTATION:
THE EXTREME METHOD@

How about getting your nagging salon problem solved so fast that you will never believe it?

Alan offers unique, bespoke and highly charge consulting calls over any medium you use (Type, WhatsApp etc). Share your most pressing issues and you are pretty much guaranteed to leave the call with a solution that is designed around your salon. One salon owners just recently have now discovered the best path to come off the shop floor and keep her staff packed out at the same time after just 60-minutes with Alan

SALON EXTREME LIVE:

Regardless of how long you've been in business, there are times when you simply want to hear something refreshing, motivating, inspiring and uplifting. All can offer bespoke talks to fit your salon very precisely.

Don't Forget Your Free Bonus!

Download FREE copy of ***How to Access and Get Back Missing Salon Clients in 15 Minutes Using Your Smartphone***

Simply visit www.salonpunk.com/imissing

Register your details, name and email address (we need them to send you the free book) and that's it.

Lightning Source UK Ltd.
Milton Keynes UK
UKHW010709010219
336544UK00010BB/396/P